The

Moral

Libertarian

Idea

2020 Updated Version

TaraElla is an author and a singer-songwriter. She is passionate about individual liberty, strong families, and healthy communities.

Visit www.taraella.com to see more of her work.

Contents

I. What is Moral Libertarianism

Moral Libertarian Perspective: Equality of Moral Agency

The principle of equality of moral agency is central to moral libertarianism, because the need to allow every single individual their equal share of moral agency underpins the moral case for liberty and liberalism. As I have previously illustrated, liberals are not the only people who allow some kind of liberty, but we are the only ones who insist that liberty be given equally to every individual, not excluding those in government. Traditional feudalism allowed kings and lords almost boundless liberty simply by inheritance, but that meant slaves and serfs did not have any moral agency over their own actions, i.e. they could not act upon their moral consciences in their lives, but rather had to obey the consciences of their lords. We liberals, and moral libertarians in particular, cannot support offering anyone the kind of liberty kings and lords once had, because that would include having moral agency over other people, which means taking away other people's fair share of moral agency. Instead, we strive for every adult to have an equal amount of moral agency, which must therefore mean that everyone has full moral agency over themselves, and only themselves. But why is this important? And what does the application of this principle look like in practice?

What Equality of Moral Agency Implies

I believe that the principle of equality of moral agency is the most important principle in political morality, because it is the only way of distributing liberty (which is one and the same as moral agency, liberty being from a political rights perspective and moral agency from a moralistic perspective) that is consistent with the fact that every human being has equal moral standing from birth, and the fact that all human beings are flawed in some ways (i.e. not perfect and not capable of knowing the absolute truth in every sense). Let's start with the equal moral standing part. In fact, the founding fathers of the United States were some of the first people to recognise this: in their words, everyone was created equal, and therefore everyone has certain inalienable rights. Inalienable is the keyword here: these rights cannot be rightfully taken away by any action of any external authority, whether the authority comes from hereditary privilege or from collective mandate. Any action that compromises these inalienable rights are morally illegitimate. To believe that every human being is born equal morally requires that liberty (and hence moral agency) is distributed equally; in other words, a failure to distribute liberty equally is morally inexcusable, unless you happen to believe that people are not born equal. Now, let's look at the fact that all human beings are flawed. Because all human beings are flawed, nobody can certainly make the right decisions every single time. To allow one human being to make moral decisions for another against their will therefore potentially means forcing someone to commit a moral wrong even while knowing it is wrong. Furthermore, allowing those in power to make moral decisions for everyone else means that, when the leader of a country doesn't get it right, the whole country commits a moral wrong. The worst example of this in all human history would be the Holocaust.

Mussolini, the Father of Fascism: He Who Does Not Believe in Equality of Humans

Now, let's look at what happens when the principle of equality of moral agency is not respected. Mussolini, the father of fascism, was a classic example of a man who did not believe in the equality of moral agency. According to Mussolini, all the individual wills of the Italian people had to be moulded into one, and in practice that meant he had all the moral agency in the whole of Italy and his people had none. This was consistent with his belief that he was some kind of superman who could do no wrong, as captured by the slogan 'Mussolini is always right'. As Mussolini thought that he was not flawed and always made the right decisions, he believed he deserved moral agency over his people because he would always make the right decisions while his people may not. But of course, this was pure hubris on his part, as in reality he was one of the most immoral human beings who ever lived, and the ideology he invented brought endless misery to countless numbers of people. To disrespect the principle of equality of moral agency, to think that one can make a better decision and hence should have moral agency over other people, is to have at least some of Mussolini's hubris. While most people who believe in forcing their morality down other people's throats are nowhere as evil as Mussolini, their hubris is just as morally unsound.

Others who Disrespect the Equality of Moral Agency: Too close to Mussolini for comfort

The most classic case of Mussolini-style moral hubris is the kind of people who think they are carrying out God's Will, and hence have the authority to do anything in their 'mission'. Since they believe their ideas and actions necessarily reflect God's Will and hence the absolute truth, they believe there is no need to allow their human beings equal moral agency. This idea is most often associated with fundamentalist religious militants, who have caused tragedy after tragedy, who have committed utmost acts of evil while believing that they were carrying out God's Will. However, similar themes can be found in some sections of the religious right in the mainstream politics in many countries, who often self-righteously attempt to frustrate democratic mandates for liberal reforms because they think they are acting in God's Will. Thinking that one's beliefs in any area is certainly in line with God's Will is the same as thinking that one's beliefs, in that area at least, is 'always right'. This pattern of thinking leads straight to Mussolini-style hubris. On the other hand, a moral libertarian is allowed to have conservative viewpoints (otherwise it would defeat the point of moral libertarianism, right?), but they would need to make their case fairly and respectfully through the free market of ideas.

But it would be a folly to think that only those on the right are capable of such moral hubris. After all, Mussolini was left-wing when he was a young man. The left may not talk much in terms of God's Will, but they do talk a lot in terms of justice. Justice means the right thing to do, and is simply the secular equivalent of God's Will. Like how some of the political religious right think that their version of morality is always God's Will, an increasing number of leftists believe that their version of justice is always actual justice. When one starts to think this way, one essentially allows themselves the right to impose one's own version of justice on others, including those who do not believe in the same version of justice. For example, when authoritarian leftists believe that free speech leads to injustice, they insist that everyone practice safe speech (as they define it), and ideas that don't accord with their version of justice are met with actions of no-platforming, sometimes violent. Some moral libertarians may well share similar beliefs to these leftists in various areas, but out of respect of the equality of moral agency, would instead do their best to make their case in the free market of ideas, hoping to persuade other people to join their cause of action, while seriously dealing with the arguments thrown up by opponents. As a result of their morally unsound approach, the authoritarian leftists end up trying to impose upon everyone programs of 'justice' that even those who would supposedly benefit from don't want, like the kind of radical feminism that most women actually reject, or the kind of intersectional feminism that is actually GLIF (gatekeeper limited intersectional feminism, i.e. where intersectional oppressions only count if you have the correct political beliefs too). On the other hand, moral libertarians

12

can continue to refine their ideas of justice through competition in the free market of ideas, gradually modifying what they offer as a result of feedback from people's lived realities, resulting in ideas that benefit as many people as possible.

Equality of Moral Agency: The Basics

So for those of us who decide that we don't want any part of Mussolini-style moral hubris, that we wish to respect and honour the equality of moral agency in every way, where do we start? First of all, we need to see our ideological opponents as having equal moral agency too. As long as they are not shoving their beliefs down other people's throats, to live and let live is our only option. No-platforming and safe speech are too fascistic to even be considered. Secondly, we need to learn to love and respect the free market of ideas. While it is a good thing to be strongly passionate about justice, we need to make our case in the free market of ideas, and treat our ideological opponents as equals in the process. We need to be open to feedback, especially in relation to people's actual lived experiences. This will make our ideological 'products' more responsive to the actual needs of individuals and families living in the real world, and make them more 'competitive' in the marketplace of ideas. Rather than seeing everything in us-vs-them (or 'class struggle') terms, we need to see the development of ideas of morality and justice as a continual process of refinement, which is facilitated by this free market of ideas, just like how the free market of consumer goods leads to the improvement of such goods over the years. Finally, we need to recognise that it is not up to any of us to determine subjectively whether each idea is progressive or 'regressive'. If an idea can thrive in the free market, it is by objective definition bringing new value to previously unserved populations and serving previously unmet needs, and is therefore progressive. If an idea is objectively regressive, i.e. it is worse than what is currently on offer in all respects and does not bring new value to anyone, it will not survive in the free market of ideas.

The Moral Libertarian: A Moral Case for Liberty and Liberalism

In recent years, it has become fashionable to look down upon liberalism. It started on the right a few decades ago. American conservatives quite successfully painted American liberals as people who are elitist, out of touch, and spend tax dollars 'liberally' just because they want to. Now this disease has spread to the left. While American conservatives still use the l-word to describe everyone to their left, resulting in ridiculous phrases like 'Bernie Sanders is very liberal' (when he won't even support free trade), a new generation of leftists have identified themselves as socialists and pit their identity against those people they call liberal, as in Bernie is a socialist, Hillary is a liberal. While the attacks on liberalism come from different angles, they share some common themes: liberals are out of touch elitists, supporters of the privileged establishment, enemy of the common good, technocrats who think they know what's best for everyone, and so on. A very sad description indeed, especially for the ideology of Locke, Mill and Burke, the ideology of both Keynes and Hayek, the ideology of such great leaders as Prime Minister Lloyd George and President Franklin Roosevelt, and the ideology of most early feminists.

Liberalism's Fall From Grace

So how did liberalism fall so far from grace? I believe the answer lies in idealism, or rather, the lack thereof. As liberalism came from the margins into the mainstream of political thought, it took on the reins of government more and more frequently. By the mid 20th century, liberalism became identified with governments, who was inevitably made up mostly by elite and establishment figures, and whose day-to-day job was mostly concerned with making practical decisions, often on the advice of technocratic 'experts'. In other words, what was once conservatism's weakness became liberalism's weakness. We can actually see that at the same time, in the former Soviet block, these establishment characteristics became lumped in with socialism. We can also see that, as western conservatives started losing their grip on the establishment, they started finding their idealistic voice again, and began to attack liberals as the new 'establishment'. Looking at the bigger picture, we can see that liberalism caught the disease of the establishment in the mid 20th century, and never quite recovered. Being in the establishment makes a movement lose sight of its ideals, and this insight may still fail to recover even if the establishment position is lost.

I think it is safe to say that liberalism is no longer the establishment, right now, to put it very mildly. As of this writing (2018), liberalism only accounts for a minority of world leaders. US president Donald Trump is surely not liberal. In fact, both conservatism and socialism are arguably stronger than liberalism at this point in history. Why? Because they have an ideal, they have a narrative. Right now, libertarianism is the only branch of the liberal tree to have anything close to a strong narrative built on strong principles. And even much of libertarianism isn't based on a moral worldview like conservatism or socialism. The moral consequences of consistently applying the Non-Aggression Principle (NAP) remains a controversial thing for many people, and libertarians have often argued their case on economic efficiency and lower taxes to avoid this controversy. I'm not making this up: some libertarians have argued that their ideology will allow people to truly follow their moral compass without collective coercion from society, while others have argued that with all property being private property, socially deviant behaviour will be effectively suppressed by the property owners acting out of their self interest. Which simply looks like, the consequences of a libertarian government will be what I want it to be. As for the form of liberalism that comes with a welfare state, it looks even worse. If welfare state liberalism is all about equality and wealth redistribution, wouldn't it be even more principled to go straight for socialism and oppose all free market capitalism outright? (Which is, not coincidentally, what many young people are doing.) For many people, liberalism simply doesn't look like a morality sound and principled way of looking at politics.

Liberalism as a Moral Worldview: The Principle of Equal Moral Agency

But is liberalism morally sound? To answer this question, we need to look at what liberalism is. Liberalism is the ideology that is primarily concerned with liberty, above all else. Socialism is more concerned with economic equality than liberty, conservatism is more concerned with maintaining tradition than liberty, and nationalism is more concerned with the future of the nation than individual liberty. Putting liberty first is the defining feature of liberalism, therefore. However, this cannot be liberalism's only feature, for liberty is also found in various forms in other ideologies. For example, in traditional feudal societies with absolute monarchies, the King had almost unlimited liberty. The lords also had an amount of liberty much greater than any citizen in a modern liberal democracy: for example, they had the 'liberty' to own and trade slaves. The unique thing about liberalism is that it aims to distribute as equally as possible the liberty of each person in society. Therefore, while nobody can have the liberties of kings and nobles past, everyone can have their fair share of liberty. While liberals disagree on how liberty can be distributed most equally, with some arguing for NAP-based libertarianism and others arguing for a strong welfare state, this often unspoken shared principle is what we have in common.

How does liberalism's dedication to distributing liberty equally make it a moral ideology? To answer this question, we need to first look at what liberty is. Liberty is the power an individual has over their own actions, their ability to put their ideas into action. Therefore, looking at it from a moral perspective, liberty is moral agency, i.e. the ability to act in accordance with one's moral compass. An equitable distribution of liberty therefore ensures an equitable distribution of moral agency. In this way, liberalism ensures that every individual in society has an equal share of moral agency. At this point, we need to turn to the fact that liberty (and hence moral agency) are also finite resources: if some have more, others must have less. If lords can command slaves (therefore having more liberty), slaves will not be able to act according to their own moral compass, and thus have no moral agency. Therefore, in an equal distribution of liberty (and hence moral agency), everyone can have full moral agency over their own beliefs and actions, but nobody can have moral agency over another. This, I would argue, makes liberalism the ONLY morally valid ideology. Since all human beings are morally flawed to some extent, allowing some humans to have moral agency over others is morally impermissible. Allowing a lord to command a slave as he pleases means that the slave must commit an immoral act even if the act is both objectively immoral (as in absolute truth) and known to be immoral by the slave, as long as the act is not known to be immoral by the lord (or alternatively he is a depraved lord and does not care). This has several consequences. On an individual level, the slave would be morally responsible (at least in his conscience, and also by the laws of religion for those of us who are religious) for committing a moral wrong, knowing that it is wrong, but not being able to resist anyway. On a societal level, it also means that those holding power can commit severe atrocities, without the moral consciences of other people acting as a brake. Which was actually how tragedies like the holocaust happened. One may be tempted to argue that, as long as we prevent having bad governments by being vigilant voters and by putting in place national and international regulations, nothing as bad will happen again. But this is naive, because the ability to judge if governments are good is limited by the fact that politicians often lie their way into power and manipulate the political landscape once in office. It is also still true that no human being can perfectly know the absolute truth of what is morally right or wrong, and therefore, if we simply let those in power decide for everyone, there will still be plenty of injustices, even if nowhere as great as the holocaust. The principle of Equal Moral Agency is the only thing that will prevent such injustices.

Liberalism's Individualism is Required by its Morality

The other thing about liberalism is that it is an individualistic ideology, i.e. it looks at individuals rather than groups of people or society as a whole. Socialism cares about the equality of social classes, and nationalism cares about the nation state as a whole, with both ideologies refusing to look at people on an individual level. In contrast, liberalism, insists that the equal distribution of liberty is to be implemented on an individual-by-individual basis. It is not good enough if, say, overall the people of Australia have the same amount of liberty as the people of Britain, if some people in both countries don't get their fair share of liberty. It is also not good enough if, say, overall working class women have the same amount of liberty as middle class men, if some people in both socio-economic groups don't get their fair share of liberty. The liberal aversion to some forms of affirmative action comes from this principle. For example, no liberal should support the 'progressive stack' speaking system used at some Occupy rallies. Furthermore, unlike in many other ideologies, the same rules apply to governments, because they are also ultimately made up of individuals. Therefore, the government cannot have more liberty to make moral decisions than individual citizens, even if the government is democratically elected, and even if they claim to make the decisions on behalf of oppressed minorities. For example, the government cannot coerce anyone to accept a definition of marriage they don't agree with, even if it had a majority mandate to do so, and this applies for all possible definitions of marriage. This is why liberals equally uphold marriage equality (like the left) and religious freedom about marriage (like the right). Another example is that liberals should support the right of parents to withdraw their children from absolutely any class they don't agree with, in public schools. Many of the aforementioned political positions have caused rifts between liberals and leftists in recent years. But we liberals must stand our ground firmly, if we are to be true to our moral worldview.

While both liberals and leftists are historically considered together under the progressive umbrella, liberalism's insistence on individual rights at every turn has always sat uncomfortably with the Left's wish for collective action on almost everything. The Left believes that collective, and often coercive, action can bring about progress much more efficiently. But this collective, coercive action is clearly in violation of the principle of Equal Moral Agency: those setting the agenda for the collective movement decide the course of action, and others have to follow for fear of ostracization or worse. In recent years, the Left's disregard for individuals' rights to have a fair share of moral agency has worryingly accelerated, as free speech has been replaced by safe speech (i.e. speech that is deemed politically correct by movement leaders), and measures like the so-called progressive stack, which clearly violate the equal right of every individual's voice to be considered, are popularized. Of course, while the Left claims to want more female, ethnic and LGBT voices to be heard, the moment one of these voices promotes an idea the leaders find 'regressive', it is shut down. As a result of this new straitjacket on leftist thinking, conformity within leftist ranks has accelerated, with those who are pro-life or have certain foreign policy views increasingly find themselves spat on by the movements they once considered their political homes. Meanwhile, the lack of a free speech culture means that feminist and LGBT movements are whitewashed to look like a homogenous whole without much dissent on key issues. The Left is clearly embarking on a misguided path.

Meanwhile, liberalism's emphasis on individual liberty and moral conscience provides a much better way forward for social justice. Liberalism encourages everyone to make their case in the free market of ideas. The morality or lack thereof of each idea can be debated freely, and with individuals having the moral agency to put their ideas into practice, time will also tell what fruit their ideas will bear. In this way, the free market effectively decides the best, most moral and most fruitful, ideas that will survive into the future. John Stuart Mill called this the cauldron of ideas, with new ideas being added into the cauldron constantly and good ones living on, but I prefer the free market metaphor because it is, to some extent, a competitive process. A brand new idea, like a brand new product in the marketplace, is usually nowhere near perfect. The process of having to compete with competitors leads to modification and innovation, and even in some cases imitation, to make for a more competitive product. In the same way, ideas can be refined, and the morality of individuals and hence the society they live in can improve with time, just like how the quality of consumer goods improve with time. Also, in this free market of ideas, there is no need to subjectively judge whether ideas are progressive or regressive. If an idea is truly regressive, i.e. worse than what is already on offer, people will not 'buy it', much like how nobody can hope to make a profit off a business selling twenty-year-old computers. If an idea is truly regressive, it will not survive the free market of ideas. On the other hand, if an idea can thrive in the free market of ideas, then it cannot be regressive in an objective sense.

The Moral Libertarian Creed

Of course, what I have outlined above is only one reason to support liberalism. Both historically and in the present, there have been plenty of other reasons for liberal politics. Mill's liberalism, for example, was strongly associated with his utilitarianism, while my liberalism clearly has nothing to do with utilitarianism. Therefore, we need a specific term to describe the supporters of liberal politics who approach it from a moralistic angle, or more specifically, those who are committed to the principle of Equal Moral Agency as their creed. I propose that we identify as Moral Libertarians. Like civil libertarians being concerned primarily with civil liberties, we are primarily concerned with moral liberty. And just like civil libertarianism, moral libertarianism does not have a fixed economic program. Civil libertarians can be anything from minarchists to socialists, depending on their other beliefs. Likewise, moral libertarians can take a variety of economic positions, depending on their views of what moral liberty should entail and how it can be equitably distributed, informed by their own conscience. Thus moral libertarianism forms a new branch of the liberal tree, overlapping somewhat with libertarianism, classical liberalism, civil libertarianism and welfare liberalism in different ways.

The Moral Libertarian Manifesto

Preamble

A ghost is hanging over the West: the ghost of liberalism. The ghost of only partly fulfilled yet already abandoned promises of life and liberty, of equality and fraternity. Liberalism is not quite dead yet, but nor is it truly alive. It can only watch hopelessly as far-right and alt-right white nationalist elements duel it out with far-left neo-Marxist tendencies, with liberty being the biggest loser of each and every battle. The right had made 'liberal' a dirty word for four decades, and now a new generation of the left is about to do the same, the two long-time enemies burying liberalism in a rare bipartisanship.

Is it too late for liberalism? No, not really. But to return to life, it will need a life force. Life force comes from conviction, from moral principles, and from confidence. Only the moral libertarian idea, with its grounding in the one simple principle of morality that has been the unspoken core of liberal thought in history, will be able to resuscitate liberalism and return it to its previous vitality. Moral libertarians seek to clearly spell out their principle of Equality of Moral Agency (EMA), and vigorously apply it and defend it in the free market of ideas.

The rest of this manifesto is structured similarly to Karl Marx's famous Communist Manifesto of 1848, not because we are Marxists, but because it is a familiar format, and the historic spread of Marxism is testament to the effectiveness of this format. We hope that the Moral Libertarian idea will spread far and wide. (We have however decided to make it shorter, because two centuries on people like reading long texts much less.)

1. What is the Moral Libertarian Idea

Liberalism is an idea with a history stemming from the Western Enlightenment. The old world of master and slave was being swept away. In its place, a long line of thinkers from John Locke onwards theorised about how we can have a structure of liberty and equality instead. Since then, much has been achieved, but as we all know, the project is still incomplete. Furthermore, since the early 20th century, the rise of new forms of collectivism have repeatedly threatened to put liberal ideas in the dustbin of history. During the Great Depression of the 1930s, many thought that the end of liberalism was inevitable, with fascism and communism being the only two choices in the future. Many fascists proudly claimed that individualism was for the 19th century; that the 20th century would be the century of collectivism. But liberty proved more resilient, and re-asserted itself in the post-war world, while fascism was largely discredited and buried once its immorality was exposed. More than half a century on, liberalism is again facing a crisis, and various forms of authoritarian collectivism are again promising utopias of various kinds. Liberalism is not as popular anymore, in a world where the dichotomy is increasingly left vs right, socialist vs capitalist, 'anti-fascist' vs 'alt-right', etc.

But it would be too soon to declare the irrelevance of liberalism once again. Why? Liberalism is the most moral ideology, and ideologies that are immoral at their core will sooner or later be discredited, like the fascism of the interwar period. Liberalism will be left standing the victor, like in the post-war period, as long as it has not been completely killed by its authoritarian opponents. Therefore, our mission is to give liberal ideals as much life force as possible. Such life force can only come with idealism, moral conviction and clear principles. We believe that the one core liberal idea is the Equality of Moral Agency (EMA), i.e. each and every individual should have equal ability to live and act out their sincerely held vision of morality, and no outside force, no matter if it is an individual despotic ruler or the tyranny of collectivist pressure, should be able to diminish any part of this. This is in fact the only morally valid structure for society, because as inherently flawed human beings, none of us are morally correct all the time. Therefore, to be able to force another to abide by one's moral values will inevitably mean forcing another to act in a way that is immoral at least some of the time. To allow this would effectively be to allow the conditions that caused the Holocaust, where thousands of people enabled the Holocaust to happen just because they were not allowed to oppose the will of Hitler. In other words, other ideologies are too similar to fascism, from a moral libertarian point of view.

Moral Libertarians argue for and uphold the principle of Equal Moral Agency at all times, on all issues, during all debates. We are well aware that we not only do not yet have equality of moral agency as things stand, the work to create a structure of equal moral agency will likely take generations to come. Each year, each decade, each generation, we strive to make things closer to the equality of moral agency, by insisting this principle be the core consideration for any policy of reform, and to encourage reform wherever we find that things are inconsistent with this principle. Bit by bit, we will be able to create a structure providing effective equality of moral agency for all. We are inherently reformist, because revolutions require there to be a strong leadership group, making this option against the equality of moral agency in principle. Furthermore, history has shown that once the leadership group is entrenched in power, it does not easily give up its extra moral agency (nor is it able to anyway). On the other hand, slow and steady wins the race.

Consistent with our core principle, Moral libertarians will strictly uphold the freedom of speech and freedom of conscience for all, and the freedom of religious belief for all. We will also strongly support reforms that remove state-sanctioned inequality of moral agency, for example marriage laws which privilege opposite-sex marriage above same-sex marriage. We will argue for the equal respect of individuals regardless of their characteristics or their political beliefs, left, right or center. We will also argue, on the same grounds, for the equal respect and treatment of all individuals, regardless of ethnic background, gender and gender identity, sexuality, and disability status. We strongly oppose on principle all discriminatory treatment, whether justified from 'conservative' grounds of tradition, or 'progressive' grounds of historical debt or disadvantage.

2. Answering Criticisms of Moral Libertarianism

Does Moral Libertarianism harm traditions and traditional morality? No, it doesn't, simply. Moral libertarians oppose the top-down maintenance of tradition by those in power, but people are free to live by, embrace and promote traditional points of view. In fact, our staunch opposition to top-down enforcement will, especially in the longer run, prove to be the greatest protector of traditional values.

Does Moral Libertarianism fail to protect minorities and excuse bigoted behaviour? No, we staunchly argue against discrimination, and are the only political faction which does so consistently. While we cannot support reducing freedom of speech, we do not believe this to be detrimental to minorities, because only open discussion will be effective in changing attitudes. Furthermore, moral libertarians uphold John Rawl's famous Veil of Ignorance in all our decision making, and thus are politically race-blind, gender-blind and sexuality-blind, while aiming to create systems that work for every single individual equally. Many of us support anti-discriminatory legislation in employment, for example, because we believe in society needing to be group-blind, as individualists.

Does Moral Libertarianism, with its encouragement of individualism, encourage selfishness and discourage communitarian thinking? Moral libertarians are opposed to the tyranny of the majority and strongly encourage individualist thinking. However, once individuals have their freedom to think and act, there is nothing preventing them from deciding to act for the benefit of the community. However, each individual will have their own right to determine what they believe is the greater good, rather than have a specific kind of greater good dictated to them by other people.

Does Moral Libertarianism neglect economic equality, especially historical economic equality? Moral libertarianism is not attached to any economic doctrine, and supports the democratic determination of economic policy, consistent with our support for democratic means of determination for every political issue that is unavoidably collective. In other words, every voter in the country should have a say. This way, we can have an economic policy that will serve the economic liberty of a broad range of people. The fact that, when the people have spoken they do not choose a certain economic policy (libertarian, Marxist, or anything in between) doesn't mean that there is anything wrong. It's democracy in action.

3. Relationship to Other Liberal Movements

Moral Libertarians explicitly state the assumption that underlies all other liberal movements, thus its worldviews and aims do not differ from any other liberal movement, at the core. The main difference is that we explicitly proclaim and live by the principle of Equal Moral Agency (EMA). Therefore, we avoid being liberal in technicality but being illiberal in practice. Left-liberals sometimes fail to challenge their further-left allies' encroachment on freedom of speech, while thin libertarians sometimes fail to challenge those who claim to be libertarian but are really Neoreaction-style authoritarian conservatives at the core, for example. By upholding the EMA, our liberalism is made stronger.

Where other liberal movements, including classical liberals, social liberals, cultural liberals, libertarians, and liberal conservatives, act according to the EMA principle, and are thus acting as truly liberal, we will support them. Otherwise, we will not.

4. Moral Libertarian Priorities for the Next Decade

In culture, we will uphold the freedom of speech and conscience for all. We will staunchly oppose any move towards so-called safe speech, and any attempts at no-platforming speakers, no matter what their political stance is. We will uphold freedom of religion for every individual, including the right to religious attire (opposing burka bans etc.), and the right to promote religious-based beliefs (e.g. the wide variety of religious views on abortion). We will also uphold the right of individuals to be entitled to express their sincerely held beliefs and truths, regardless of race, gender, gender identity or sexuality. Therefore, we support multicultural liberty (e.g. the choice of singing competition contestants to sing in a foreign language every week if they wish to), and we support LGBT liberty (e.g. the liberty of any gender expression without negative consequences from society). We will discourage everyone in society from taking cultural opinion personally or adopting a victim mentality, because this will be bad for rational discourse in the free market of ideas.

In politics, we will advocate for the removal of state-sanctioned privileges on both grounds of individual privilege and cultural value privilege, including unequal marriage laws and adoption laws, and work regulations that unfairly impact religious minorities, for example. We will also advocate for strong action to protect the sanctity of free speech and the prevention of so-called safe speech and no-platforming from becoming the new norm.

II. Why Moral Libertarianism?

Reviving the Full Spirit of Classical Liberalism: Individual Liberty Plus Community Building

In recent years, there has been an apparent revival in popularity of 'classical liberalism'. The ideology of great 18th and 19th century thinkers like John Locke, Adam Smith and John Stuart Mill appears to have become fashionable once again. However, it also appears that there is no clear consensus on what 'classical liberal' means in the context of the 21st century. The term has been adopted by minarchist libertarians, moderate conservatives, and old-school JFK-style (i.e. pre-1968) liberals alike, people who clearly have very different political views on certain important matters. It is clear that there is no unified definition of 'classical liberalism' in the 21st century.

And to a large extent, that's only to be expected. Political and economic conditions today are very different from back in the 19th century, and it's practically impossible to put the ideas of thinkers like Smith or Mill directly into practice in today's context. What people are doing in each case is basically extracting what they see as the most important elements of classical liberal thinking, and applying those elements in contemporary political practice. And it's just natural that different people would see different parts of the classical liberal heritage as more (or less) important than the other parts, which would cause great differences in how they would apply that heritage to today's issues. Of course, there are also core features of classical liberal thinking that are essential in any contemporary interpretation, for example the importance of free speech. Which is why contemporary 'classical liberals' of the left, right and centre alike still have some things in common, for example a staunch defense of free speech.

While not detracting from the aforementioned observations, I wish to offer my view of what I find most important and inspiring about the classical liberal tradition. For me, classical liberalism's heart and soul does not lie in dogmatic ideas like small government or any bill of rights. Rather, it is about maximizing individual freedom. Which is why, I believe, the best way to practice classical liberalism in the 21st century, in the full spirit of its values, is to consider each issue in the light of whether the proposed solutions would offer an equal and maximum amount of freedom to each individual. I believe that the classical liberal way would be to choose the solution that would offer the closest approximation of this ideal, in every case and every circumstance. Moreover, we should do this on an issue-by-issue basis, so that in every area of life we can get as close to this ideal as the contemporary circumstances would practically allow. Furthermore, we should revisit previously settled issues periodically, to examine if the circumstances have changed due to, for example, technological advancement, so that we can now further improve things to get even closer to the ideal of equal and maximum liberty for all.

Finally, classical liberalism has always been about building better communities and societies too. It is simply not true that classical liberalism is about selfishness or 'greed is good' (a common smear from those on our left), or about the wholesale abandonment of traditional values (a somewhat common smear from those on our right). After all, none of the great classical liberal thinkers wanted to build a society that is selfish, greedy and lack morals. Instead, classical liberalism both creates the conditions required for a strong and coherent society in natural conditions of diversity, and also allows individuals to use their creativity and their moral conscience to help strengthen and improve society, by contributing their best into the free market of ideas. The liberty and equality inherent in the classical liberal tradition allows communities to be strong yet diverse in its thinking at the same time; and allows new ideas to be explored while traditions to continue to grow at the same time. Seen through this light, classical liberalism is not only not a selfish ideology; it is the best foundation for community building, especially in the contemporary age. I believe that, to revive the full spirit of classical liberalism, this community building aspect of it should be promoted and highlighted more often.

Moral Libertarianism Avoids the Core Weaknesses of Conventional Libertarianism

In recent years, there was a wave of popular support for political libertarianism that came, peaked, and then ultimately crashed. That wave came with the 2012 Presidential campaign of Ron Paul, probably peaked around 2014, and probably already crashed in late 2015 or so, as the primaries for the 2016 US Presidential election started heating up.

Back in 2014 or so, there was high hopes that libertarianism would finally break through during the 2016 US elections, perhaps through the candidacy of someone like Rand Paul. Alas, this was not to be. Instead, 2016 saw both the revival of paleoconservatism with the candidacy of Donald Trump, and also the revival of socialism with the candidacy of Bernie Sanders. Both tendencies have since taken over the political conversation in much of the West, in a way that libertarianism simply failed to. I guess we really need to ask the question, why did libertarianism fail where paleoconservatism and socialism succeeded, even when libertarianism actually got a head start.

I think the problem is simply that, political libertarianism, as it exists, simply does not speak to the needs and desires of most people. Libertarianism does not provide a clear path towards fulfilling both personal needs, such as jobs and health care, or societal needs, such as a strong social fabric and strong family values. Most people prefer non-libertarian politics simply because they feel like it would deliver what they want more effectively, and unfortunately, it is probably true at least in some cases. Purist libertarians may lament that this prioritization represents either stupidity or a willingness to submit to tyranny among the general population. However, whatever one's judgement of the situation may be, it remains a fact that classical libertarianism has not been able to advance the cause of liberty in any practical way in the real world, simply because it cannot win enough hearts and minds. That is why, if libertarianism is to have a positive effect on the real world, it must change. After all, in the game of democracy, it is never the voters who are wrong; it is always up to those who want to make their case for change to adapt.

This is where Moral Libertarianism is superior to conventional libertarianism. Where conventional libertarianism puts the emphasis on cutting the size of government, Moral Libertarianism simply aspires to every individual having equal and maximum moral agency in every situation. For example, where having a particular social program benefits so many people that most people would strongly support it, conventional libertarianism would still oppose said program on principle due to the need to cut government at every turn, even if this would represent political suicide. Furthermore, a blanket opposition to all social programs is bad for community building, which is required to create the strong social fabric only under which individual liberty becomes sustainable. On the other hand, Moral Libertarianism recognizes that having a social program, having a slightly larger size of government, does not necessarily prevent every individual having equal and maximum freedom. The Moral Libertarian might allow or even support said social program, as long as it is administered in a way that respects the ideal that every individual should have equal and maximum moral agency, or in other words, the program does not cause the freedom of the individual to shrink. This way, Moral Libertarianism can be flexible enough to allow beneficial social programs, and still aim to preserve individual liberty by keeping the administration of such programs honest to the core ideals of classical liberalism.

Furthermore, back when classical liberalism was founded in the 18th and 19th century, the big business establishment did not exist yet, and the only threat to liberty was government tyranny. Hence, limiting the reach of government was the main work of freedom fighters back then. However, capitalist society has developed through many stages since then, and nowadays the ability of the rich and powerful to take away the freedoms of other individuals has become a much bigger threat to liberty compared to two centuries ago. A politics of freedom that does not have a mechanism to restrain the rich and powerful, particularly the corporate establishment, is going to sound outdated or even insincere to many people in the contemporary situation.

Hence, conventional libertarianism's sole emphasis on restraining government at all costs, and its phobia towards restraining other parties via regulation, severely harms its credibility in the eyes of many. On the other hand, the Moral Libertarian approach would be to simply consider whether every individual gets to have equal and maximum liberty, or as close to that state as possible. Moral Libertarianism recognises that, where government is preventing liberty, it should be restrained. However, it also recognises that, where other parties are limiting the liberty of individuals, they too should be restrained. I believe that this approach is a much more credible approach to securing liberty in the context of the 21st century.

Reconnecting Libertarianism and Communitarianism in the 21st Century

Libertarianism is all about individual liberty. Communitarianism is all about building strong communities. Libertarianism sees the key to human thriving in individual freedom. Communitarianism sees the key to human thriving in strong families, healthy communities, and shared bonds. With all these differences, libertarianism and communitarianism have sometimes been seen as opposites. However, they are actually not incompatible at all. In fact, they are complementary, with one enhancing the other.

While libertarianism prizes individual liberty above all, the fact is that individual liberty does not exist in a vacuum. Using a simple example to illustrate the point, in societies and times where there is a complete break down of social order, there is no room for individual liberty. In such situations, the basic need of security is required to be satisfied first, and in prioritizing safety and security above all, individual liberty is inevitably sacrificed. Likewise, where the social fabric is diseased and social trust is very low, people will also prioritize security and sacrifice liberty. Furthermore, the 'free market of ideas', as well as the whole process of free debate and democratic decision making, would become distrusted by many people, which would lead to the devaluation of associated values like free speech. The fact is, individual liberty is simply unsustainable without the right social environment. The project of communitarianism, in putting an emphasis on strong families, healthy communities and a strong and healthy social fabric, creates and maintains the social conditions under which individual liberty can thrive. This is why libertarianism ultimately needs communitarianism.

On the other hand, a community can only be strong if there is mutual respect and a healthy level of mutual trust between its members. This requires that there be as little 'power play' as possible, a condition that is effectively achieved if (and only if) there is maximum liberty for every individual, so that nobody can wield massive power over anyone else in any case. Furthermore, for a community to serve the needs of its members effectively over time, its culture must be adaptive. This would be achieved only where there is free debate for every issue. Finally, to ensure long term harmony among people with diverse values and ideas, everyone should be allowed to 'do their thing' as much as possible, as long as it doesn't harm another's right to do similarly. As we can see, for a communitarian project to be successful, especially in the longer term, a strong and fundamental respect for individual liberty is required.

The fact is, individual liberty and community building need each other. A libertarianism without communitarianism is unsustainable, and so is a communitarianism without libertarianism. This is why we must stop entertaining the notion that libertarianism and communitarianism are somehow opposites. The two ideals are stronger when they are linked together.

III. Moral Libertarianism vs Other Perspectives

Should a Moral Libertarian Always Support Smaller Government?

Political libertarians, by definition, always support reducing the size of government. The political libertarian application of the non-aggression principle (NAP) requires that taxation be kept to a minimum, and therefore the size of government be kept to a minimum. But just like how civil libertarians can sometimes be, but not always are, political libertarians, moral libertarians also are not always politically libertarian. This is because civil libertarians and moral libertarians both focus on one aspect of liberty that is not predominantly economic, while political libertarians emphasize mostly economic liberties and property rights. Therefore, while political libertarians always support smaller government, it is not a foregone conclusion that the same applies to all moral libertarians. But, in reality, should moral libertarians support smaller government?

Moral Libertarians are not always Political Libertarians, because the Economy is a Complex Thing

Since moral libertarianism is necessarily based on the principle of the equality of moral agency, whether a moral libertarian should strive for smaller government also depends on whether smaller government is more consistent with the equal distribution of moral agency or not. For some moral libertarians, the answer is simple. Since they believe that the NAP is the ultimate expression of equal moral agency (since nobody can initiate aggression against another), the full application of the NAP is, in their opinion, the closest we can get to having equality of moral agency. Therefore, supporting immediatist libertarian politics, i.e. cutting government by as much as possible, and right now, is a logical conclusion. Other moral libertarians also see great compatibility between the NAP and equality of moral agency, but recognise that the immediate application of libertarian politics could lead to outcomes where some people's basic liberties (and hence moral agency) could be in a worse situation than is the case right now. Hence they advocate a gradualist libertarian politics. Still others believe that, since the power to coerce people does not solely reside in the government in modern society, the government should be maintained at an adequate size to counter other potentially coercive forces, like gross economic inequality. Again, within this camp, opinions about the adequate size of government can differ. Hence, there is no one single answer as to if moral libertarians should support smaller government.

And that's OK. Because moral libertarianism is ultimately about respecting the equality of individual moral consciences, people are allow to differ in their consciences, and make their case in the free market of ideas. Since each political state can only have one government, the size of government is an unavoidably collective matter. In my opinion, where matters are truly unavoidably collective (i.e.

not just conventionally collective like the definition of marriage), every concerned individual owns a part of the matter, and where equal moral agency is respected, a democratic method of decision making (as close to one person, one vote as possible) should decide the outcome. Therefore, in my opinion, moral libertarians should make their case about the appropriate size of government to promote equal moral agency, and should also participate in the democratic process as guided by their individual consciences. It really doesn't matter that moral libertarians will therefore not be voting the same way as each other because, unlike the left, we do not believe in collectiveness in action, except where people have genuinely voluntarily agreed to.

More on the Liberal Debate about the Size of Government

Modern American commentators like to divide liberals into 'classical liberals', who supposedly believe in the absolute right to private property like modern libertarians, and 'modern liberals' or 'social liberals', who spend tax dollars liberally to solve society's problems. In fact, that's not even close to the truth. Even John Locke, often considered the father of classical liberalism, stressed that while society should respect private property rights there should be enough and as good left over for everyone else, a sentiment clearly incompatible with sections of modern libertarianism who believe that all property should be private. Also, John

Stuart Mill and Prime Minister Lloyd George supported some wealth redistribution, with the latter raising taxes while in office. Liberalism has always strived to balance property rights with other factors that affect the liberty of individuals.

My personal inclination is towards having a government that is large enough to support a strong social safety net, but as limited as possible beyond that. While a government too big will be tempted to use its powers to coerce individuals (thus violating the principle of equal moral agency), a government too small may mean third parties effectively have the power to coerce individuals, for example via economic means. There needs to be a balance somewhere in the middle. In my opinion, a government that provides a moderate welfare state particularly in healthcare, education and looking after the unemployed, but otherwise respecting the free market and international free trade, as well as private ownership of industries, provides the best balance. I am also a libertarian gradualist, in that I believe the size of government should be reduced when it will no longer adversely affect anyone's liberty as a result, and we should strive to make this situation a possibility in the longer term.

What About Social Issues?

While moral libertarians do not always have to support smaller government in an economic sense, we do need to stay true to the principle of equality of moral agency when it comes to cultural and moral matters. In my opinion, governments should be as neutral as possible in cultural and moral controversies. Here, the role of government is to maintain the free market of ideas, by maintaining the rule of law and the safety of individuals, so people can speak up without fear. The government taking sides is generally incompatible with respecting the equality of moral agency, because that would mean individuals making decisions in the government (e.g. presidents, prime ministers, members of parliament or congress) having greater moral agency than private individuals. Even if the government takes sides based on majority mandate, it would still mean that individuals with the majority view have greater moral agency than individuals with the minority view. Unlike the economy and national security, most cultural and moral issues are not unavoidably collective, and should be de-collectivized as much as possible so that individuals can truly have equal moral agency over these issues. It is due to this reason that I support marriage privatization, for example. In this sense, I do believe that moral libertarians should mostly, if not always, support smaller government.

Is Moral Libertarianism Compatible with Conservatism? (What does it say about abortion?)

I have written a few other pieces examining if moral libertarianism is compatible with various ideologies (e.g. thin libertarianism, thick libertarianism, welfare liberalism, socialism). However, conservatism is yet another important ideology with lots of followers, and probably the most popular ideology worldwide at the moment. Hence, we need to answer the questions: is moral libertarianism compatible with conservatism? Can conservatives work with moral libertarians? Can one be a conservative and a moral libertarian at the same time?

Conservatism is a political ideology that has both economic and social aspects. Since moral libertarianism is actually compatible with any economic ideology as long as it is justified on liberty, and conservatives justify that small government economic philosophy on liberty, there is nothing incompatible here. Therefore, the rest of this article will focus on the social issues.

Moral libertarianism insists on equally distributing liberty, and hence moral agency, among every individual in society. Therefore, as moral libertarians, we insist that every individual be able to live according to their moral compass, as long as they do not infringe upon others' rights to do so. As promoting conservative ideas and living according to conservative values does not infringe upon any other person's moral agency, moral libertarians cannot be opposed to this kind of conservatism. In fact, moral libertarians have a responsibility to defend the right of conservatives to live according to their moral compass. While moral libertarianism does not say anything about abortion, for example, it says that everyone must be able to live according to their values on this issue. Therefore, moral libertarians absolutely support and defend the right of conservatives to voice their opposition to abortion under any circumstances, without social penalty. Furthermore, moral libertarians absolutely support and defend the rights of pro-life health professionals not to be involved in abortions.

On the other hand, moral libertarianism's principle of equal moral agency also means that no person can make cultural or moral decisions for another person. Therefore, we oppose government enforcement, and even encouragement or discouragement, of any worldview or lifestyle, and support ending such paternalistic actions where they have traditionally occurred. This means we cannot accept some aspects of traditional conservatism. However, traditional conservatism's reliance on government intervention to uphold tradition actually assumes one thing: that they have the ability to do so. In a democracy, that would mean the conservative position has majority support. Evidently, this is not always the case, especially in the West in recent decades. Throughout history, when conservatives had majority

51

support, they often used government power to enforce their morals. But this actually creates a precedent, allowing other groups to use government power similarly in the future. Hence, part of the modern conservative experience is to fear leftist authorities refusing to leave conservatives alone to live their conservative lives. A switch to the principles of moral libertarianism will effectively prevent this from happening.

Conservatism is also not a monolithic thing. People who wish to uphold tradition may choose to 'adapt' differently, in the face of changed circumstances. For example, while most conservatives oppose same-sex marriage at the moment, former UK Prime Minister David Cameron famously said that his support for same-sex marriage was due to his conservative values. If you happen to believe that marriage equality is key to preserving the relevance of marriage as an institution for the future of humanity (like I do), then you would naturally see the majority conservative position as actually aiding anti-marriage radicals on the far-left. Members of conservative parties around the world who hold this view (but are not in leadership positions like Cameron was) are often pressured to stay silent. In contrast, moral libertarians believe that everyone should be equally able to make their case in the free market of ideas, allowing all views to be heard.

In conclusion, moral libertarianism provides plenty of space for conservatives to both promote their values and live according to their moral compass. While we have no choice but to oppose old-school conservative governments' sometimes paternalistic policies, the other side of the same coin means that we will always defend conservatives' right to their own moral agency against those leftists who believe that people should be pressured into going with their program. This is actually quite a good deal, especially given that modern conservatives can no longer be certain that they always have majority support.

Moral Libertarian Perspective: All Social Engineering is Morally Unsound

Almost everyone say that hate social engineering. Many people hate social engineering with a passion, and for good reason. Most people's gut reaction to social engineering is that it is unfair and tricky, somewhat like rigging an election. For moral libertarians, who believe in the equality of liberty (and hence moral agency), social engineering is unconditionally unacceptable, because it means that those doing the engineering are making important decisions, often moral decisions, for the subjects of the engineering. Wherever there is social engineering, there is no respect for the principle of equal moral agency, and hence no respect for the equality between humans. From a moral libertarian perspective, social engineering is simply immoral.

Another thing about social engineering is that it is much easier to oppose social engineering designed to achieve outcomes you don't like. For example, conservatives are good at spotting the slightest leftist slant in public education curricula. But the same people would often justify pro-conservative social engineering, such as government policy that favours heterosexual relationships over homosexual relationships, as either upholding tradition or upholding the will of the 'silent majority'. This is actually a double standard, because social engineering is still social engineering, even if it has been carried out for hundreds of years, and even if it is supported by the majority. From a moral libertarian perspective, the principle of equal moral agency is still violated, because the individuals making decisions in government are still making moral decisions that all other individuals in society must accept, even if against their own will. The government is still the moral master, and the people are still the moral slaves. In fact, if those supporting conservative viewpoints truly believe that they have the unwavering support of the majority, they really do not need the government to uphold anything. If they allow the government to step aside from governing the moral sphere, private individuals will regain their fair and equal share of moral conscience, and conservative individuals (which conservative politicians believe are the majority) will be able to live out their conservative beliefs by personal example, much more effectively than when government interference exists.

The left is similarly blind when social engineering favours their worldview. While the left is generally unsympathetic to social engineering for the sake of preserving the status quo, they are much more sympathetic to social engineering that will supposedly promote equality of outcome. In many leftist circles, free speech is becoming increasingly rare, and policed speech is increasingly becoming the norm. So-called safe speech is often justified on the need to protect the feelings of minorities, but in reality it is a form of censorship, that effectively disallows certain ideas from entering the free market of ideas (or John Stuart Mill's cauldron of ideas if you prefer that analogy). Even if you start with, for example, the seemingly clear-cut rules of only prohibiting racist and homophobic speech, it effectively sets a precedent that can potentially disallow political speech promoting pro-life ideas (because it hurts the feelings of women who had abortions) or cultural expressions that are deemed to be cultural appropriation (because it hurts the feelings of people who don't wish to see cultural appropriation). And once it becomes acceptable to ban political speech and cultural expressions, there really is no limit to what else can be banned. A Stalinist dictatorship is the only logical conclusion.

Another worrying recent development is the prioritization of people's right to speak, based on their personal characteristics. This was first seen in the 'progressive stack' speaking system that was used in some Occupy rallies, where women and minorities were afforded priority in their right to speak. This system clearly sees people as members of groups rather than individuals, in a way not unsimilar to how old-school socialism saw people as solely members of their economic class, or how fascism saw people as solely members of their nation and their race. In the name of achieving some sort of group-based equality, the principle of equal moral agency between individuals is sacrificed. Furthermore, as the progressive stack is a social construct invented and maintained by leaders of leftist movements, it is a system in which they decide the rules, it is therefore by definition a system in which the leaders have much more moral agency than anyone else. From my personal experience, it is not uncommon for those who have the right to decide who is to speak to use their power to favour those who will say what they want to hear. In recent years, I have heard from an increasing number of women and LGBT people complaining that they have been excluded from systems and institutions that are supposed to be inclusive, because those running the system don't like to hear what they have to say. (Those running the system often like to counter that people who promote 'regressive' ideas are to be excluded. However, this definition of 'regressive' is a subjective one, and often bears no relationship to the more objective definition of regressive I use, i.e. does not bring any new value to anyone beyond what has already been offered. In fact, I often suggest that, if an idea really meets the aforementioned objective definition of regressive, it will be rejected in the free market of ideas, so we don't need to do anything about it.)

p.s. A particularly worrying feature of leftist social engineering is that it is often inspired by theories arising from sources like philosophy, sociology or feminism. While I believe it is important for people to critically reflect on the state of our society, and many such theories have given us useful language and frameworks to discuss important issues, the theories themselves are almost always far from flawless, to put it mildly. In fact, I make this observation about history: although progressives have been the winners throughout history (because, by definition, only new ideas can change the course of history, restating old ones cannot), progressives of any era only get a minority of things right, and more progressive ideas eventually get rejected than accepted. The French revolution's Liberty, Equality, Fraternity lived on, but their revolutionary calendar did not. Similarly, 19th century socialists played a very important role in highlighting the injustices of early capitalism towards the working class, but their demands to nationalize industries have been largely rejected. Karl Marx's prediction of the collapse of capitalism has not come true either. This is not to say that the investigation of society and the production of progressive ideas is not worthy. It just highlights the need for such ideas to be tested and refined in the free market of ideas.

Moral Libertarian Perspective: Genuinely Free Markets are a Moral Imperative

Ever since the Global Financial Crisis, it has been fashionable to blame the free market for everything. This, in turn, has caused a substantial number of people to believe that, if the free market can be abolished or at least severely constrained, it would be to the great benefit of humanity. In this political climate, those who espouse anti free market ideas certainly don't lack ears willing to listen. But is the idea of a free market really that bad? Or is abandoning the free market really a good idea?

First, let's start with the moral libertarian perspective. The moral libertarian answer on this issue is clear: moral agency (and hence liberty) must be distributed as equally as possible. Since the only alternative to having a free market is having a government controlled market (as in a command economy), the only way to abandon the free market is to allow the government to have decision making powers far beyond that of private citizens. Therefore, to oppose free markets in practice always means violating the principle of equal moral agency. It logically follows that moral libertarians must support free markets. Moral libertarians can differ on how a genuinely free market can be maintained, for example regarding what role the government may play in stabilising economic conditions and providing equal opportunity for all, or if any and what kind of anti-trust and competition regulations there should be. But there is no way a moral libertarian can oppose the free market and still stay true to the principle of equal moral agency.

But let's not talk in terms of abstract principles, because facts are more persuasive for most people. There has never been a liberal democracy that has also not had some form of free market economy. While there are countries with free markets but not liberal democracy, there has never been a country with liberal democracy but not free markets. In other words, although it isn't necessarily true that the freer the market, the freer the people, where the markets aren't free, the people certainly aren't free. In fact, the early history of the USSR illustrates why this is the case. Lenin wanted to abolish private property and free market capitalism, but was not able to do so completely. The much more hard-line Stalin put in place a program of compulsory collectivization, which of course led to massive resistance, especially from peasants whose land were being confiscated. Stalin, of course, crushed all resistance ruthlessly. The lesson is that, since people are not going to voluntarily give up their economic interests, anyone hoping to control the economy would need to be as much of a ruthless dictator as Stalin. Of course, Stalin had to control more than just the economy. As he became deeply unpopular, he had to also disallow political dissent to protect his rule, so that his program of collectivization could continue. This demonstrates why you cannot abolish the free market economy without also abolishing political, and hence social and cultural, freedoms.

The free market of economic goods and services is also ultimately inseparable from the free market of ideas. In command economies, goods can only be produced and sold with the government's permission. This means the choice of goods and services available is strictly limited by the government. Whatever goods the government doesn't like, it can effectively ban. At this point, we need to keep in mind that some goods are cultural or political, for example books and movies. In fact, historically, those who controlled the printing press controlled knowledge and opinion. Similarly, a command economy unavoidably gives government the power to control knowledge and opinion in society.

The recent backlash against the free market economy has to do with its perceived unfairness. I actually believe that this point is worth discussing. Traditionally, those who believe in a market with minimal intervention have claimed to be the truest and purest champions of the free market. Hayek and his followers famously claim that they do not care if people start in a position of equal opportunity, and that social justice is meaningless. But the moral libertarian perspective actually provides an alternative view of what a free market should look like. Moral libertarians primarily believe in the equal distribution of moral agency. A moral libertarian's free market would therefore require that people have equal opportunity, for the market to be truly free. In my opinion (again, not necessarily the collective view of all moral libertarians), this equal opportunity may be provided by a combination of public education, welfare for the unemployed, and anti-trust and competition regulations to ensure that new players can enter the market. As for the classic Austrian School argument that this would be too much government intervention in the economy, for the free market economy to exist and function continuously, there already needs to be a substantial amount of government intervention anyway. For example, the government needs to issue and maintain a stable currency, there needs to be a reserve bank, there needs to be laws against fraud, there needs to be a police force to keep people's private property safe from thieves, and there needs to be a military to keep the nation secure from being taken over by external forces. Extreme libertarian 'solutions' like private currencies, private police forces and private militaries remain a pipe dream, and in any case could never provide the investor confidence needed for the free market to function properly. Given that the government already needs to be a substantial size just for the market to function, increasing it by a relatively small amount (public education and unemployment benefits are cheaper than the military) to make it even more of a free market (in the moral libertarian view) can be well justified. As long as the government doesn't start setting prices, restricting international trade or nationalizing our banks and industries, it is still a free market.

Ensuring free market economies also provide equal opportunities is not just a moral libertarian imperative. It is also a very practical imperative, for those of us who want free markets to survive. It is very easy for people like Hayek to say that they do not care about equal opportunity and social justice. But for those who are actually prevented from participating meaningfully in the free market economy from birth, it is very difficult for them to believe in the free market system. It is these people who anti-market 'revolutionaries' find their audience and supporters in. Therefore, a free market with equal opportunities is also a strong and sustainable free market, and a market that doesn't care about equal opportunity essentially doesn't care about its own survival.

It Takes Bravery and Commitment to be a Moral Libertarian

Moral libertarianism sounds simple. And it really is. After all, it's simply about making sure that everyone has equal moral agency. And the only practical and logical way to do that is by allowing everyone maximum liberty to live according to their moral compass, and not allowing anyone the 'liberty' to prevent others from living according to their moral compass. A really simple concept that can be easily applied to almost all social issues out there (economic issues are often a bit more complicated).

Unfortunately, it isn't always easy to uphold moral libertarian principles. The classic case concerned opposition to unjust wars. For most of human history, when leaders of a country have declared war on another country, for any citizen to dissent was almost akin to treason. No amount of religious moral conviction was enough justification for allowing dissenters to speak up. Fortunately, this all changed somewhere around the 1960s, triggered by the Vietnam War. On a more everyday life level, social pressures still exist in many circles, limiting the political stances one can publicly take without social penalty. For example, after 15 years of fighting for marriage equality, I still find it difficult to raise the subject with many friends and family members.

The left in the West, ideological descendants of the enlightenment, has traditionally been a reliable champion of free speech, and the Free Speech Movement of the 1960s was instrumental in finally allowing dissent in a wide range of areas, most importantly regarding whether a war is just. However, in recent years, parts of the Western left have walked away from free speech, instead preferring an approach where people's feelings come first, the so-called safe speech. This climate has made staying true to moral libertarian principles very difficult indeed in some leftist circles. Throughout history, conservatives have sometimes made dissent a crime against loyalty, religion or traditional values. But making unpopular opinion a crime against individuals' feelings is indeed a new concept the moral libertarian has to defeat.

A moral libertarian must speak up according to their true beliefs, and must resist peer pressure to shut up. But since the moral libertarian wants everyone to be equally able to speak up freely, we must also aim higher. It is unrealistic to expect everyone to be willing and able to resist peer pressure in the way we do, taking social penalties left, right and center as a result. Therefore, we need to strive to change the culture itself. We need to bring about a culture where it is everyone's right to speak as they sincerely believe. We also need to promote the idea that people should not take offense in the face of disagreement.

Of course, just to bring about such cultural change would put us into conflict with much of both the right and the left. I have to say that it is not a particularly friendly climate out there for us right now, for parts of the right still believe in controlling language to preserve traditions (hence, for example, their opposition to marriage equality), and the left is increasingly walking away from liberty and rationality towards group-identity and feelings. But if we believe in the ideal of equal moral agency and a genuinely free market of ideas, there is no alternative but to face the opposition and make our case.

Moral Libertarian Perspective: Why Identity Politics is Often Morally Questionable

Despite its controversial reputation, identity politics appears to be increasingly influential recently. Maybe the arrival of the new wave of feminism, or perhaps the increased awareness of racial disparities in society, is causing this identity 'awakening'. While I'm personally not a supporter of the identity politics way of looking at things, even I have to agree that identity politics sometimes helps to advance the rights of minorities. However, we also cannot overlook the fact that identity politics as it currently exists is problematic. But how is it problematic? And can we save the best features of identity politics while rejecting the problematic elements?

From a moral libertarian perspective, initially there appears to be no problem with identity politics per se. If everyone had equal moral agency, surely some individuals can use their moral agency to advance the rights of the minority group they belong to? There is surely nothing wrong with this. However, things are really not that simple. Identity politics, in practice, often means seeing the world in an in-group vs out-group perspective. This perspective can lead some to only care about the rights and liberty of the in-group, and diminish the need of people outside the group for similar rights and liberty. This us-vs-them mentality doesn't sit very well with a commitment to distribute liberty and moral agency equally among every human being.

In recent years, the rise of what I would call critical theory-ism has made identity politics even more problematic. Critical theory-ism is also often called cultural Marxism, but I will avoid that term here because it also refers to a right wing anti-Semitic theory about the Frankfurt School. Besides, critical theory-ism is really not similar to real Marxism in substance, even though it borrows a lot of Marxist language. Basically, critical theory-ism borrows the concepts of class consciousness and class struggle from old-school socialism, but applies these concepts to cultural and identity groups. Thus, women can be seen as an oppressed class, and so can LGBT people or ethnic minorities, and they should 'struggle' against the privileged classes (white, male, heterosexual, and so on). Like how some old-school socialists advocated taking away the rights and liberties of the bourgeois class at least temporarily so that the working class could be liberated, many critical theory-ists have no problems with reverse discrimination, as it's just all part of the 'class struggle' and 'liberation'. Critical theory-ists also demand that good allies in the privileged classes should 'check their privilege', which often includes accepting unfair treatment without complaint. If these supposedly privileged people dare voice concerns about being treated unfairly or vote at elections in a way that they think will end the unfair treatment, they can be labelled right-wing and reactionary. In fact, what I just said could make me a counter-revolutionary enemy in the eyes of critical theory-ists. An us-vs-them, all out culture war thus begins. (Meanwhile, I understand that actual socialists and Marxists are also upset at this situation, because for them class solidarity is the most important thing, and the division of the working class into identity sub-groups is to be strongly discouraged.)

Anyone who is not stupid can see that there can be no compatibility between the critical theory-ists' version of identity politics, and the moral libertarian principle of equal moral agency. Moral libertarians believe that every individual in society should have equal moral agency (and hence liberty and political rights), regardless of their identity or cultural characteristics. A woman must not have less moral agency than a man, but then a man also must not have less moral agency than a woman. Therefore, a woman must not have less liberty or political rights than a man, but a man must also not have less liberty or political rights than a woman.

However, all this does not mean that moral libertarians cannot have some kind of politics informed by the lived experience of minorities. Unlike Marxists, who stress class solidarity above individual experience, or fascists, who stress national unity above individual experience, we liberals are individualists, i.e. we care most about the individual. Individual liberty, individual needs and individual lived experience serve as the ultimate guide for a truly liberal politics. Liberalism encourages each individual to make the most of their potential, and live their lives according to their own moral compasses. Therefore, it also encourages individuals to identify systematic barriers that prevent them from doing this. It is under the umbrella of liberalism that women, ethnic minorities and LGBT individuals first found the justification that they too deserved equal liberty and equal opportunity, and found the language to express it. While conservatives, socialists and nationalists alike dismissed their concerns as selfish demands that should give way to collectivist objectives, our liberal forerunners listened carefully and helped introduce reforms to make society more liberal for everyone. And in this best tradition, we should continue to listen to what minorities have to say. As moral libertarians, we should not rest until there is equal liberty, equal opportunity, and hence equal moral agency between every individual in society, no matter what minority characteristics they may have.

In fact, the liberal version of identity politics, which is all about letting minority voices and lived experience inform us of how to build a more liberal society for all, is much more effective in being truly inclusive than the us-vs-them, culture-as-class struggle version of identity politics. First of all, when we start to think of people collectively as groups rather than as individuals, a group dynamic builds up, where individuals in the group are expected to have primary loyalty to the group. This loyalty often effectively includes following the political agenda of the group leaders. Thus pro-life feminists often find it difficult to have a place in predominantly pro-choice feminist movements. Similarly, politically conservative or even centrist LGBT individuals often find themselves unwelcome in some activist groups led by socialist leaders.

Thus such movements end up not serving all women or all LGBT people, they only serve those who politically conform to the activist establishment's wishes. First and second wave feminism often prioritized the needs and experiences of white women, and dismissed the voices of black, Latina and Asian women. Hence the introduction of intersectional feminism. But as much of feminism still has gatekeepers, the agenda of this so-called intersectional feminism is still limited by the agenda of the gatekeepers, making it effectively a Gatekeeper Limited Intersectional Feminism (GLIF). In the liberal version of identity politics, none of this would occur because everyone is welcome to add their voice to the free market of ideas; there simply is no group and therefore no leaders or gatekeepers. Secondly, group-based identity politics not only creates unequal moral agency between groups, it also creates unequal moral agency within groups. Those who do not conform to the activist establishment's agenda effectively have less moral agency, because they are often discouraged from speaking up or even semi-coerced into changing their views. Their disfavoured position within the movement also means that they may be excluded from activities of decision making. Thus they experience injustice within the movement itself, which further compounds the injustice they receive from the wider world as a result of their female or minority status. Unlike the group-based approach to identity politics, the liberal approach stresses equal liberty and equal opportunity for each individual, thus by design it will never make people excluded in this way.

IV. Some Moral Libertarian Ideas

The Moral Libertarian Way to Social Justice

In an encouraging development, there has been an increased focus on social justice, both economically and socially, in recent years. As a liberal, I see this focus on providing equal opportunity for all as a good thing. However, I do have strong reservations about the approach of some activists, and these reservations have intensified in recent years. As a moral libertarian who believes in the equality of moral agency as the most important morality imperative in politics, things like so-called safe speech, no-platforming, political correctness, progressive stack speaking systems, and the exclusion from movements of people who express opinions the activist establishment label as 'regressive', are clearly not things I can accept. All these represent the activist establishment making cultural and moral decisions that other people are pressured to accept in one way or another, and in many cases also represent a top-down distortion in the free market of ideas.

In fact, I believe that sticking to the principle of equal moral agency is the route towards true social justice for all. After all, social justice is essentially another way of saying equal opportunity for all. Equal moral agency and equal opportunity are essentially the same thing. On the other hand, whenever the principle of equal moral agency is violated, there is not a situation of equal opportunity by definition.

From a moral libertarian perspective, things like no-platforming and the progressive stack are actually against social justice by definition, because they clearly violate the equality of moral agency. This is because, if some people can speak their minds but some cannot, or some people are given a higher priority to speak than others, there is clearly no equality of moral agency. But let's approach this from a more facts-based approach. To improve social justice, we need to know the injustices that are actually happening, and to obtain this knowledge we need to let people speak up about their lived experiences and their grievances. Not allowing some people to speak or placing them last in the queue effectively prevents them from getting the social justice they need. Back in the 1960s, college students started a Free Speech Movement, so they could voice injustices in relations to the Vietnam War and conscription, civil rights and women's rights. In time, these voices changed society forever. If conservatives were able to no-platform these activists, none of that progress would have happened. The New Left back then understood the importance of free speech. It is very regrettable that the current generation of leftists do not share this attitude.

Some leftists believe that they can subjectively classify certain ideas and attitudes as regressive, and censor them out, while not affecting social justice. In reality, this is not only misguided, this is moral hubris. From a moral libertarian theory perspective, this represents the activist establishment making cultural and moral decisions for everyone else, deciding what they can say or think. Therefore, the principle of equal moral agency is clearly violated. But this is not just an issue in theory. In recent years, I have increasingly heard from women, ethnic minorities and LGBT individuals that have been excluded from so-called progressive movements because of certain beliefs they held or certain things they said. The activist establishment's decision to no-platform ideas they see as regressive actually has the effect of turning away some of the very people they are supposed to help. If we look at it from an intersectional perspective, it gets worse. For example, ethnic minorities, whether black, Latino, Asian or indigenous, are more likely to be religious and hold traditional viewpoints, and this also applies to female and LGBT members of ethnic minorities. Furthermore, the radical solutions proposed by the activist establishment often provoke intense backlash in ethnic communities and the developing world, causing ethnic minority women and LGBT individuals to favour more moderate solutions. It is therefore unsurprising that those complaining of exclusion are very often ethnic minorities, the very people intersectional feminism is supposed to help. In fact, if intersectional feminism is practiced this way, it is not real intersectional feminism, but GLIF (gatekeeper limited intersectional feminism).

The liberal alternative is to let the free market of ideas select the best solutions for social justice, and also improve ideas concerning social justice over time. In a truly free market of ideas, solutions that fulfil the previously unmet needs of individuals will survive and thrive. Such solutions are progressive by definition, whether the activist establishment like them or not, because they fulfil a previously unmet need. A good example is same-sex marriage, a solution to a previously unmet need (the commitment and legal protection of same-sex couples) which was subjectively seen by the then-LGBT activist establishment as regressive (because they saw it as assimilation). As same-sex marriage was a progressive idea by definition (since it fulfilled a previously unmet need), it gradually won over more and more support in the free market of ideas, despite the bitter opposition of some establishment activists. On the other hand, ideas that do not offer anything better than what has already been previously offered are, by definition, regressive, just like if a company decided to sell a computer based on 20-year-old hardware and software. In a truly free market of ideas, we do not need to fear such regressive ideas, for they will eventually be eliminated by the market due to a lack of 'buyers'.

The free market of ideas also allows the development of the best solutions that will provide justice for the largest number of people over time. This is because, as differing and sometimes contradictory ideas enter the 'market' and compete against each other, proponents of ideas will have to be receptive to criticism and suggestions from other parties and improve their ideas over time so that they remain competitive. This effectively encourages repeated cycles of thesis-antithesis-synthesis, evolving and refining our ideas over time. Another great feature of the free market of ideas is that it allows minorities within minorities a better opportunity to ensure that any solution for justice also serves them well. Where a minority is seen as a homogenous group and its voice is whitewashed by the activist establishment to sound uniform, the needs of minorities within minorities are usually not well heard or considered. But where there is a genuine free market of ideas, where ideas can flow freely without gatekeepers being able to erect barriers, minorities within minorities can make their case just like everyone else, and the activist establishment will either be forced to change to accommodate their needs, or face being discredited in the free market of ideas.

The free market of ideas, being made up of many minds, each understanding their own part of the human experience, can effectively process a vast amount of information about the injustices that are occurring out there, and select the best solutions that can improve a wide variety of injustices at the same time. On the other hand, movements controlled by elite activist establishments often focus only on what people in the establishment can see, resulting in solutions that do not serve the people they are supposed to serve. Using an economic analogy, the free market of ideas is like a free market of goods and services, where complicated information about demand, supply and costs is efficiently synthesized into appropriate prices that do not cause a surplus or shortage of goods. On the other hand, the elite activist establishment is sort of like the centrally planned command economies that used to exist, where the plans seldomly met the actual needs of the people, resulting in either a surplus or a shortage of goods.

Moral Libertarian Perspective: The Thin vs Thick Libertarianism Debate

In recent years, libertarianism has become increasingly divided between thin libertarianism and thick libertarianism. Thin libertarianism only focuses on greatly reducing the size of government, upholding property rights, and upholding the non-aggression principle (NAP), and is generally agnostic on all other issues. Thin libertarianism does not care about what attitudes people out there hold about social issues, and does not care about whether social liberties actually increase or rather become more restricted as a result of libertarian policies. Thick libertarians believe in the same governmental policies as thin libertarians, but they also insist on culturally encouraging everyone to adopt a live and let live attitude, and to rid society of traditional prejudices like racism, sexism and homophobia, so that individuals in society can truly experience an increase in liberty.

While moral libertarianism is not the same as political libertarianism, and indeed moral libertarians do not have to be, and are indeed sometimes not, political libertarians, moral libertarianism shares some of the core ideology and historical cannon of thought with political libertarianism. Therefore, moral libertarians can certainly be inspired by debates in political libertarianism, and vice versa. Looking at the matter from a basic perspective, it would appear that moral libertarianism shares some of the attitudes and goals of thick libertarianism. In particular, unlike thin libertarianism, both thick libertarianism and moral libertarianism share a concern about increasing individuals' liberty in practice. I believe that there is a lot in thick libertarian thinking that can inspire moral libertarians in this area, and vice versa. In fact, on social (non-economic) issues, moral libertarianism and thick libertarianism often take similar views.

Thin libertarians often accuse thick libertarians of taking the same stance as the increasingly authoritarian 'new left' on social issues. It is not uncommon to hear from conservative-minded thin libertarians accusing thick libertarians of having cultural Marxist sympathies. I believe that the moral libertarian principles, particularly the equality of moral agency (EMA), can help illustrate why the aforementioned observation is wrong. I have written extensively on how moral libertarianism almost never actually takes the same stance as 'new left' socialism on social issues. In fact, when explaining and promoting moral libertarian positions, I have encountered plenty of hostility from the left, thus proving how different our views really are. Moral libertarians support everyone in society having equal moral agency, i.e. to live as per their own moral compass, and oppose any kind of moral coercion. Therefore, by definition we have to oppose traditional prejudice taking away the fair share of liberty and equal opportunity due to women, racial minorities and LGBT individuals. However, an important thing is that we also hold the same attitude towards religious conservatives, for example, again because by definition we have to. We believe that the religious conservative should be able to hold, promote and live according to their views concerning marriage without prejudice from the rest of society under any circumstances, for example, and this right should have no expiry date. I don't think many 'authoritarian leftists' would hold the same view.

Thin libertarians also sometimes accuse thick libertarians of promoting social views that will inevitably lead to bigger government. For example, they sometimes say that thick libertarians promote libertine attitudes that cause family breakdown and increase drug and alcohol use, which will end up causing more welfare dollars to be spent, and therefore also more taxation. This kind of attitude is actually inconsistent with the general tradition of liberalism and libertarianism, in that we should not support restricting liberty just to pre-emptively prevent social consequences we may not like. Otherwise, it would be not be liberalism, but conservatism, socialism or something similarly authoritarian. Also, there is nothing under thick libertarianism that does not allow one to promote family values and clean living. Moral libertarianism goes even further: it insists that conservatives should have just as much right to promote their views as everyone else, without any social penalty.

In fact, a lot of conservative thin libertarians' accusations towards thick libertarianism betray their lack of faith towards liberty, towards what choices people would make if given full moral agency over their lives. There are even so-called libertarians who savour the prospect of a future where the complete division of the world into privately-owned gated communities (most if not all owned by conservatives, according to their logic) will mean that most people will live according to conservative rules, not because they want to, but because they are forced to by the property owners. How is this different from authoritarian conservatism? Both political libertarians and moral libertarians can support conservative positions, but they must still respect other individuals' equal liberty and moral agency in the process. Just like everyone else, conservative libertarians can make their case in the free market of ideas, and try to persuade more individuals to live the way they want. Nothing more, nothing less.

Moral Libertarian Perspective: Political Leadership is Overrated

In these times of uncertainty and crisis, there have been repeated calls for political leadership from many quarters of society. It is as though if our politicians would make some top-down decisions for us, everything will be alright again. Of course, those calling for political leadership from different parts of the political spectrum expect really different kinds of decisions to be made, so in reality, no political leader can hope to answer all these wishes for leadership satisfactorily. In fact, a leader that can unite the country and make strong decisions that most people can accept has always been an unlikely thing. Former US President Ronald Reagan was arguably the most popular Western leader in recent decades, but plenty of people strongly disliked him and his policies. Furthermore, the dream of unity behind a 'strong leader' is becoming increasingly impossible with the increasing fragmentation and polarization of our political landscape. But, a more fundamental question is, is this the right dream to have, in the first place?

At this point, I should perhaps declare my position upfront. As a moral libertarian who believes in all individuals having an equal amount of moral agency, I simply do not believe in governments and political leaders making top-down decisions for all. Therefore, of course I don't believe in all society uniting behind a strong leader. I do not believe in political leadership for most issues, simply. But since people with ideological beliefs must still try to make their case in the free market of ideas using facts and ideology-neutral logic, in the rest of this article I will focus on just that.

Those calling for political leadership usually do so for two reasons: 1) either they want something fixed but don't know exactly how to, or 2) they want certain things fixed a certain way, but believe that only a government can do it. In fact, political leadership may seem the most immediate solution for both scenarios, but it certainly isn't the best solution for either.

If you want something fixed and your first thought is to call on the government to provide a solution, it effectively means that you trust the 'wisdom' of politicians more than your own wisdom, your family and friends' wisdom, and your neighbours' wisdom. However, history has shown this to be an often incorrect call. In fact, since all human beings are imperfect, the politicians are bound to get some things wrong, and even if just by chance, you, your family and friends, and your neighbours are bound to get at least some of these same things right. Therefore, placing your trust in politicians is effectively letting other people make decisions for you, even though you could have done better yourself. Furthermore, politics is too often a game of power struggle, alliances and deceit, and politicians may make decisions that are not truly guided by their conscience. Placing your blind trust in politicians is something only fools do. Instead, the free market of ideas, being made up of the collective wisdom of many minds competing against each other, will always provide a much better solution.

More commonly, people call for political leadership because they think they need the power of government to change things. In many cases, however, this lack of ability for change outside government is because governments have appropriated certain powers for themselves at some point in history, power that they should not have had in the first place. In many cases, community-driven change, inspired by solutions selected from the free market of ideas, would have provided both a more effective solution, and a smoother and quicker path to change, if not for the government being a roadblock. For example, governments decided that they should have monopoly control over marriage around the 18th century or so. Fast forward to more recent times, and any change to marriage laws, whether it be the introduction of no-fault divorce, or the inclusion of same-sex couples, have become something that needs government approval. Hence these issues also needlessly became political issues, and often political footballs used by politicians for various purposes. If the government had never appropriated marriage for itself, the community could have resolved these issues simply by vigorous debate in the free market of ideas. Therefore, next time you come across an issue that looks like it can only be solved by the government, you should think about if it is really that the government should give up some of its control over society and individuals.

Another area where government intervention is often called for is education. Specifically, what should be taught in our public schools forms a large part of the ongoing culture wars. Just in the West in the past ten years or so, there have been calls for and against things like environmentalism and climate change, indigenous history, colonial history, feminist and LGBT history, LGBT acceptance, competing versions of citizenship education, and competing theories of Darwinian evolution and intelligent design to be taught in public schools. In fact, so that governments and public schooling could be as value-neutral as possible, it should always be wrong to use public school teaching to advance any ideological agenda. Public schools should stick to teaching uncontroversial things, uncontroversial meaning almost universally accepted by consensus in the particular field of study. For example, Darwinian evolution is uncontroversial within the context of Biology, but some parts of feminist history remain controversial in the wider field of history. Proponents of views and theories still considered controversial should refrain from trying to make it into school curricula; they are instead welcome to spread their ideas in other ways. Under this doctrine, there should be much less need for 'political leadership' in what schools teach.

In conclusion, I strongly believe that asking for more political leadership is misguided. Instead, we should reflect on what further areas the government could give up its control, and let individuals and society have more freedom.

Moral Libertarianism is a Cultural Movement

Moral libertarianism looks like just another political ideology on the surface. It is a certain way of justifying a political attitude, liberalism, after all. A lot of what I have written about moral libertarianism references political history and political philosophy. However, I would actually consider moral libertarianism even more of a cultural movement. That is, the cultural aspects of moral libertarianism are perhaps even more important, and even more profound, than the political aspects. Let me explain.

Moral libertarianism is all about the equal distribution of liberty, and hence moral agency. Politics really needs to be changed for this to occur. However, politics alone cannot bring about this equality. If liberty and hence moral agency is to be equally distributed among each individual, without anyone having power over another, society will have to undergo an overall cultural change.

Let's start with free speech. Free speech is an inherent requirement of moral libertarianism, because if one is to have full moral agency over themselves, one needs to be able to at least voice their moral ideas without restriction. Free speech has theoretically existed in most of the West for quite a long time now. But I have to stress, it is only free speech in theory. Otherwise, there wouldn't have been a need for the Free Speech Movement, as recently as the 1960s. In the recent Australian Marriage Law Postal Survey, the No camp felt that it was less socially acceptable to voice their opinions. But my feeling was that the Yes camp actually felt more of this pressure, especially in areas where No won, even if only by a moderate margin. Either way, it shows that neither camp fully believed that they could say what they believed, wherever they were, without any social consequences. In fact, free speech does not really fully exist, where people can be easily offended by the difference of opinion. Instead, people need to be able to think rationally and resolve differences of opinion peacefully and rationally. Changing this culture of easy offense should be a big part of moral libertarians' work going forward.

Another reason why free speech could be effectively restricted is because expressing unorthodox opinion can bring discrimination on oneself in many parts of society. The sociological term for this phenomenon is the Overton Window. Ideas within the Overton Window can be socially acceptably expressed, those outside the window cannot. Over time, the Overton Window can shift, for example acceptance of homosexuality was outside the window a century ago, but is now firmly inside it. Since expressing ideas outside the Overton Window can come with a personal cost, most people refrain from doing so. Therefore, the existence of the Overton Window phenomenon means that there is not complete free speech. Again, moral libertarians should seek to change this, perhaps by expanding the Overton Window rapidly until there is no longer anything outside it.

Furthermore, the political aims of moral libertarianism can only be achieved with concurrent cultural change, including most importantly the way we think about government. While a few liberals and libertarians throughout history have flirted with the idea of having a non-democratic but very liberal governance, hypothesizing that where governments do not have to bend to democracy they can be more liberal, history has actually shown that democratically elected governments are the only species of liberal government. This is not surprising, as non-democratic governments need to maintain their rule against popular pressure, and suppressing dissent is almost always required for that. Furthermore, under moral libertarianism and the principle of equal moral agency, unavoidably collective decisions should be decided as close to one person, one vote as possible, and only democracy is compatible with this. Therefore, liberals have to support democracy, and work towards governance that is both liberal and democratic. Since in democracies, things are decided by majority mandate, if we want a liberal governance under a democratic system, we need to try our best to persuade our fellow citizens to take up liberal attitudes of thinking. If we are not successful in this, we will not succeed in any of our political aims. With the rise of the idea of 'illiberal democracy' in some parts of the world, as well as the increasingly collectivist attitude of some parts of the Western left in recent years, promoting liberal ideas about the role of government is of particular urgency in every Western democracy.

One important way moral libertarians can promote liberal ideas about governance is to promote methods of change that do not require government intervention. For example, if we want to raise awareness about certain issues, don't ask for the government to include it in the public school curriculum. Instead, use blogs, social media and word-of-mouth. Of course, where those with opposing ideas want to use governments and public schools to advance their agenda, we should consider that cheating, and protest strongly.

Moral Libertarian Perspective: The Question of Private Property

NOTE: This article represents ONE moral libertarian's thinking on the issue of private property. It does not represent all moral libertarians' thinking on this matter. In fact, I accept that moral libertarians can be as pro-property as Rothbard or as anti-property as Marx, as long as their case rests on liberty, because moral libertarians must accept the equal moral agency of each other.

Is private property good for liberty? Modern political libertarianism's answer on this issue is clear. For most contemporary political libertarians, whose thinking have been most strongly influenced by the views of thinkers like Hayek, Rothbard and Nozick, liberty means absolute private property rights, and where private property rights are even just a bit compromised, there is no true liberty. On the other hand, socialists and social liberals (left-liberals) claim that it would mean those who have no means of acquiring private property, most often due to being born into poverty in the first place, are effectively left without even basic liberties. In fact, their line of argument is also backed by historical thinkers, from Rosseau to Marx, who believed that private property should be abolished for the sake of liberation. A third approach is that of John Locke, often considered the father of classical liberalism. While Locke strongly supported private property rights, he thought that there also needs to be enough and as good left over for others to use. This is clearly quite different from some modern libertarians, whose ultimate visions involve every part of the world being held as private property without exception.

Let's start from the modern political libertarian view, because that seems to be the default position in the discussion about property and liberty. Modern libertarianism is based on the non-aggression principle (NAP), which holds that no individual can commit aggression against another under any circumstances, unless they have broken the law through aggression against another in the first place. It logically follows that the government cannot take away any individual's private property under any circumstances, because, even if an individual refuses to pay taxes, they haven't committed aggression against any third party, and therefore the government dragging them to jail at gunpoint for refusing to pay taxes violates the NAP. However, this view of property rights is ultimately impractical, because no matter how small the government is made, some amount of taxes still have to be paid, and where the government jails individuals for not paying taxes it would still violate the NAP, meaning one could argue that the NAP-based property rights logic ultimately leads to anarchism. Furthermore, other people may argue that this logic depends on a particular definition of 'aggression'. For example, taking another view, merely trespassing into private property is not an act of aggression, therefore neither the government nor property owners should be able to use violence to prevent trespassing. Allowing law enforcement against trespassing but not allowing law enforcement against tax evasion thus would be a double standard. This logic essentially leads to no effective property rights for anybody! It is therefore not surprising that the vast majority of people do not see the NAP as a practical basis to resolve the issue of property rights.

(Several libertarian thinkers have proposed that property owners instead be able to hire private police services and private militaries to protect their property. But firstly, such services would be very expensive, and out of the reach of the average property owner. Secondly, the authority of a private police service would not be recognised by another, resulting in such services acting like rival gangs where there are disputes. Investing in the wrong police service would therefore result in loss of property. Police services with proven track records will also therefore be able to raise prices to sky-high levels. Therefore, in the real world, there is no alternative to government regulation to maintain property rights. Leftist anarchists are at least right about one thing: no government, no private property, and no free market capitalism either.)

But let's imagine a society there the NAP approach to property rights has taken hold. Every bit of the world is now privately owned. People are born into vast privately-owned lands, sort of like the nation states that used to exist a few centuries ago. Since every bit of this land is owned by the CEO, he makes all the decisions, and the people who live there have to obey his orders, or else face eviction, probably into some wasteland near the North Pole that nobody wants to own. Those who disagree with the CEO and can afford to rent property in another CEO's land can move, but those who cannot afford to move must just obey. In fact, at one point in history, people lived in similar circumstances: it was called the middle ages. In this kind of world, there is very little liberty for the vast majority of people. If this is your ideal world, then you might actually fit right into the Neo-reactionary crowd. But for us moral libertarians, there is clearly nothing like the equality of moral agency we so insist on here. In fact, it demonstrates why John Locke, though a strong supporter of property rights, believed that there must be enough and just as good left over for everyone else.

Now, let's think about another solution: what if there was no private property? This could theoretically be achieved overnight by the government simply refusing to enforce property rights. If, at the stroke of the clock at midnight the government stopped enforcing property rights, what do you think would happen? Chaos would probably take over by five minutes past midnight, with thugs breaking into properties and taking what they want everywhere across the country. After all, it's legal now. Of course, in this kind of society, there wouldn't even be basic safety and security for most people, let alone liberty and equal opportunity. In fact, there are several places around the world right now which are experiencing a total breakdown of law and order, so one does not even need to imagine how such a society would look like. I don't know anyone who would like to live in one of those places.

Thus, when the far-left proposes there be no private property, they don't generally mean the abolishment of all regulation of property rights. Rather, they seek to collectivize the ownership of property as much as possible, using their own words. But what does this collective ownership look like? How can I collectively own a house, for example, with the four million other people who live in the same city? Who gets to decide what can be done about the house? Or even who can live there? Of course, to answer all this would require heavy-handed regulation from the government. In fact, in practice, collective ownership has always meant government ownership, because no other form of collective ownership is practically possible. Where the government owns all the property, they effectively have all the liberty and moral agency, because they get to make all the decisions: not unlike the kings and nobles of centuries past! Modern western democratic socialists often insist that, where the government is democratic, the decisions are effectively made by the people. But anyone with any experience in politics can tell you that politics is a game of powerplay, where alliances, strategies and deceit is the order of the day, meaning that 'representative' democracy is not always truly representative. Short of having a referendum on every decision to be made, there is no way to ensure that every decision truly reflects the will of the people. Therefore, a lot of the moral agency of making political decisions still rest on the hands of the politicians themselves. Giving government too much power effectively means that politicians have a lot more moral agency than private citizens, something that is unacceptable from a moral libertarian point of view.

But let's pretend that property can be effectively collectively owned, for example via a government that somehow always makes decisions according to the majority's wishes. In this way, all the collective decisions would be made by the collective moral agency of the people without the politicians having any extra influence, in line with moral libertarianism's demands. But moral libertarians should only support collectively making decisions that are unavoidably collective, because these issues metaphorically represent one single indivisible pie of which everyone owns an equal share, and the only way to make a decision about what to do with this pie that respects equal moral agency is by each person having an equal share of the decision. However, many issues are not unavoidably collective, and moral libertarianism demands that each person be able to make their own moral decisions and live accordingly. Extending the pie metaphor, everybody has their own pie, and should get to decide what to do with their own pie, and only their own pie. Here, collective ownership is incompatible with moral libertarianism, because if all pies are collectively owned, the majority also gets to decide what the minority can do with their own pies. Thus in any moral controversy, the majority, being the majority, have moral agency over everyone in a winner-takes-all fashion, and the minority have no moral agency at all. This kind of democracy would essentially be an illiberal democracy. Thus, even where collective ownership is possible, it would result in illiberal democracy at best.

Having looked at all the possible solutions for property rights, we can come to three conclusions. Firstly, private ownership of property is a necessary condition for liberty and equal moral agency, because 1) if there is no protection of private property, as in anarchism, then the physically strongest will rule over everyone else; 2) if all property is collectivized (i.e. government owned) politicians will practically rule over everyone else; 3) even if we could collectivize property in truly democratic way the majority in any dispute will effectively be able to take away all liberty and moral agency of the minority. Secondly, property cannot be too unequally distributed, because that will mean the haves can rule over the have-nots, effectively replicating the feudal system. Thirdly, there is really no objective reason why a government that maintains a system to protect private property via laws and policing cannot also demand some taxation for the purposes of wealth redistribution, as without government regulation in the first place private property cannot practically exist! If governments already tax individuals to maintain their private property (courts, militaries and police forces are expensive to maintain), and in the practical world owners of private property have to rely on this system to enforce their property rights, why can't the system be designed to include some wealth redistribution to ensure a more equal distribution of private property, and thus ensure actual liberty for all?

Moral Libertarian Perspective: Power, Oppression and Liberation

Political philosophers throughout history have pondered questions of power, oppression, and how to liberate people from oppression. In recent years, such topics have also entered mainstream consciousness in an unprecedented way. There's one thing everyone can agree on: wherever there is power, there is great potential for oppression. And as Foucault and many other philosophers have noted, power and power dynamics are to be found everywhere in life. (I disagree with Foucault on a lot, but at least he understood this.) Therefore, oppression is potentially everywhere. However, just how to liberate people from oppression is still one thing that we cannot find consensus on yet.

I believe the moral libertarian principle of equal moral agency should be central to any sincere attempt to liberate everyone from oppression. Under the principle of equal moral agency, nobody can have power over anybody, and hence there is no oppression. In other words, as long as we strive to achieve the principle of equal moral agency, we will be heading in the right direction to liberate everyone from oppression.

It is also therefore, the more we care about liberating everyone from oppression, the more we must oppose everything that runs contrary to the principle of equal moral agency. To this end, we must oppose all government policy deciding top-down for everyone that certain citizens shall be second class and afforded less rights, for example laws against the religious freedom of certain religious groups, or laws against the equal rights of LGBT individuals. We must also oppose structures that allow some people to control what others can say (or even preventing them from speaking up in the first place), like so-called safe speech and the so-called progressive stack. For those who believe in true liberation from oppression, there are should be no excuses for refusing to uphold the principle of equal moral agency.

Some conservatives may argue that certain 'traditional' policies are needed to uphold tradition, or to stop what they consider to be the left's 'long march through the institutions'. However, they clearly have too little faith in the free will and moral compass of the many individuals that exist in every society. Would they just sit there and allow a 'long march through the institutions' to occur? In fact, if somebody wanted to initiate such a 'long march', they would most likely start with the government, and then use government power to forcibly change every other institution. Weakening the ability of governments to define societies certainly prevents this approach.

On the other hand, some progressives argue that we need to give certain groups priority to speak up, and remove the ability of other groups to have a voice, to achieve equality. This view not only doesn't respect individuals as individuals rather than just members of groups, this view is also deeply misguided from a power and liberation perspective. Because such arbitrary systems by definition require policing by certain individuals, they effectively help create a power differential, and hence great potential for oppression. Some may think that this temporary inequality will help end oppression, but this idea has never worked in history. Rather, it just changes the oppressors to people who happen to identify as 'progressives'.

In conclusion, sticking to the principle of equal moral agency is the only way we can head in the right direction to end all power dynamics and oppression. Anything else is simply 'some are more equal than others', and will inevitably create dynamics of power and oppression.

The Moral Libertarian Case Against Victim Mentality

Traditionally, almost every culture had discouraged victim mentality, i.e. the worldview of oneself as a victim of external circumstances, and instead encouraged everyone to adopt a can-do attitude. The downside was that the protests of those on the receiving end of very real injustices were generally dismissed. Possibly as an overreaction to this history, nowadays some progressives are effectively encouraging women, ethnic minorities and LGBT individuals to adopt a victim mentality. Of course, this more than solves the traditional problem of dismissing protests against injustice. But going too far in the other direction may also have unintended consequences.

Don't get me wrong. We need to recognise the actual injustices that are happening out there, so we can remedy the situation. Encouraging minorities to speak up about the actual injustices they face in their lives can provide all of us with much needed insight. However, when one's identity and worldview is almost defined by being a victim of forces beyond one's control, that is what I would call having a victim mentality. With the recent increasing popularity of identity-based 'socialism', where the concept of class consciousness is extended to cultural 'oppressions', and where everyone is competing to claim less privilege, victim mentality has never looked so cool. However, a victim mentality is not only personally disabling and psychologically unhealthy, the widespread adoption of victim mentality can have severely adverse consequences for liberty. Since we are talking about moral libertarianism here, the rest of this article will only deal with society-wide consequences.

Having an all-encompassing victim mentality inevitably colours one's cultural and political worldview too. Feeling like a victim all the time naturally makes one desire, and even demand, protection from 'stronger' people. This creates a justification for those who think of themselves as the protectors of oppressed minorities, giving them licence to police the speech of other people. Any dissent can then be labelled as bullying or victimization. Hence, victim mentality and free speech are mutually incompatible. Furthermore, from a moral libertarian point of view, this is totally unacceptable, because it effectively means one is making moral decisions for others, even if it is justified on social justice and protection.

Those with a victim mentality worldview are also at risk of developing a mutually oppositional, us-vs-them worldview. When one thinks of certain groups in society as their oppressors, it is easy to think of them as enemies. Fears of giving the 'oppressors' any chance to 'oppress' also loom large. Thus, it becomes easy to see personal liberty and opportunity as a winner-takes-all 'competition' between forces of good and evil, where for the 'oppressed' to thrive, the 'oppressors' must have as little liberty as possible. Literal equal opportunity becomes unacceptable because this would give the 'oppressors' opportunity to harm the 'oppressed'. It is therefore unsurprising that people who think this way often have no problems with reserve discrimination and even, in some cases, reverse oppression. Of course, this way of thinking is also incompatible with the moral libertarian goal of equal moral agency for all.

I am not saying that pursuing justice and standing up for minorities isn't important. But there are ways to do so without encouraging people to adopt a victim mentality. We can instead lead by example and tell the world that we stand against bigotry and discrimination, because we are not as cowardly as those who cannot face their own prejudices. We do not need 'safe speech', because we are confident of the rational righteousness of our position. We are confident that our position will win in the free market of ideas, and with reason bigotry and hate will be defeated once and for all.

In conclusion, the rise of a culture of victim mentality is not something liberals, and particular moral libertarians, can accept. Victim mentality is not only uncool, it is dangerous for the future of all humanity. There are better ways to bring about social justice.

Moral Libertarians should Fight Political Correctness from both Left and Right

Many people say they hate political correctness. Of course, moral libertarians naturally hate political correctness too. The principle of equal moral agency requires that everyone be able to express and promote their moral views, which means that free speech is needed. Furthermore, we believe in the free market of ideas, which requires a lack of impediment to free speech to function properly.

Among people who say they hate political correctness, however, many fail to oppose all forms of political correctness, or worse, fail to even recognize all forms of political correctness. For example, in last year's Australian Marriage Law Postal Survey, the 'no' camp said that extending marriage rights to same-sex couples was political correctness. But was that really true? After all, same-sex couples already lived in committed relationships recognised by society, and often had legally unrecognised wedding ceremonies. Same-sex couples already lived in marriage-like relationships, and their relationships were generally regarded across Australian society as not different in nature from heterosexual marriages, as evidenced by the landslide victory of the 'yes' camp. Hence the idea of marriage being a relationship between two people regardless of gender was already de-facto correct, it just wasn't legally correct, i.e. politically correct. Amending the law would bring legal and political correctness in line with the reality. Conversely, the idea that marriage could only be between a man and a woman had already become only politically correct, because it did not line up with lived reality in Australian society anymore. Hence, the 'no' camp was the politically correct camp, hoping to maintain a standard of political correctness that deviated from reality. As you can see, conservatives are not free from political correctness either, they are just blind to it: so blind that they often accuse the other camp of being politically correct instead.

In fact, the left is also responsible for some of the right's attitude that political correctness is whatever they don't like. A substantial part of the left have bought the idea that political correctness is who they are, so much that when former Democratic presidential candidate Bernie Sanders blamed Donald Trump's victory on political correctness, the comment were controversial within the left. In this case, the political correctness Sanders was referring to surrounded the lack of criticism of pro-corporate policy in mainstream media and politics, something both socialists and libertarians alike have been complaining about for quite a long time. Therefore, there was no reason why the left would disagree with him here. In fact, the left didn't disagree with Sanders at all, they were just not used to describing their opponents as politically correct. But Sanders was clearly correct here. Mainstream politics had presumed a 'correct' point of view and failed to represent other points of view, and this is political correctness by definition.

Having discussed two examples of right-wing political correctness, I believe I need to provide some balance here. Of course, the left is not without problems of political correctness either, to put it mildly. In recent years, the left has indeed taken leftist political correctness to new heights, with concepts like no-platforming and safe speech. Politically incorrect speech is now deemed unsafe, and must be no-platformed, i.e. completely disallowed. This attitude, formerly believed only to exist in fascist dictatorships, is invading progressive circles at a worrying pace. Reviving the free speech culture and upholding the free market of ideas has arguably become our most urgent imperative, as moral libertarians. As a former US president liked to say, freedom is never more than two generations from extinction.

In conclusion, political correctness comes from both the left and the right, and perhaps even other directions too. To oppose political correctness sincerely is to oppose all forms of political correctness consistently. We cannot allow being against political correctness to become just a brand politicians use to attack opponents, or a slogan the right use to attack the left.

Why a Moral Libertarian must not be Utopian

Some people have asked me: is moral libertarianism a utopian philosophy? After all, we don't have anything remotely like equal moral agency yet, and we aren't likely to get there in the next decade. My answer would be that an ideal that we can work gradually towards is, by definition, not just a utopian dream. It is an ideal that will take generations to work towards, but we are making good progress. Looking back a century ago, for example, would reveal that people have a lot more equal moral agency today compared to back then. As long as we keep the ideal alive and let it guide our reformist path forward, we will gradually get there.

Moral libertarianism is, in fact, incompatible with utopianism of any kind. Why? Someone's utopia must necessarily be different from another's. Under the principle of Equal Moral Agency (EMA), nobody will be allowed to implement their own version of utopia. Instead, everyone will have to settle for compromises when it comes to collective issues. Thinking about it, allowing anyone to implement their own version of utopia will necessarily be oppressive to those who disagree. Therefore, moral libertarianism removes this possibility for a good reason.

Which brings me onto my next point: moral libertarianism is necessarily evolutionary and reformist. A revolutionary program can never be compatible with the principle of Equal Moral Agency, when you think about it. Revolutionary action requires collective action, and such collectivism necessarily requires the extensive obedience of individual wills to the collective will. Where the individual will is in the minority and hence is opposed to the collective will, the individual will lose moral agency, which is instead given over to those representing the collective will, i.e. the majority. Moreover, revolutions generally require strong leadership, and in that case the leaders have a lot more moral agency than anyone else. History has taught us that once people have too much moral agency over others, it will be impossible to make them relinquish it without yet another revolution, which may create the same problems over again.

Revolutionary socialists in particular have aimed to challenge moral libertarianism by pointing out the lack of actual equal moral agency where there remains gross economic inequality. And in this, I do not argue that they are wrong, at least in the situation of our current reality. As previously mentioned, equality of moral agency is an ideal to work gradually towards, rather than to demand overnight. In my opinion, we have two options going forward to deal with this problem: firstly, to reduce and eventually eliminate actual poverty, and secondly, to reduce and eventually eliminate the extra influence that 'money can buy'. Both of these areas are important focuses of both political and socio-cultural reform. Moral libertarians prefer this gradualist approach because it is the only one that will bring us the results we want in the longer term. A revolutionary approach can never bring equal moral agency in the end, because it has to set up situations of unequal moral agency as a means to bring about revolutionary change. On the other hand, reformists work things through the liberal democratic system, and therefore are already building a situation of equal moral agency bit by bit with each debate and each reform. The debate of individuals in the free market of ideas is the inherently liberal way to progress, after all.

Furthermore, revolutionary socialists generally advocate for the abolishment of all private property and the collectivization of everything as part of their revolution. As I have said elsewhere before, a society where everything is collectivized allows no individual will, because the collective will is needed to approve of almost any action. It must necessarily follow that there will be a tyranny of the majority, where those in the majority will have all the moral agency, and those in the minority will have next to none.

The exact reformist path towards a state of equal moral agency is not yet clear. However, I believe that if we uphold this principle in every single issue and reform we consider, we will get there gradually. After all, history tells us that letting an ideal inspire gradually unfolding reform, as seen in the liberal evolution of British society for example, is a much better way than setting up a grand narrative of history and

111

forcing that narrative onto reality, as is the case in many (failed) revolutionary movements.

On the other hand, I believe we should always be on guard for any attempts to roll back the equality of moral agency that we have already achieved. Therefore, any attempt to deliberately introduce inequality of moral agency, whether from the left or the right, should be seen as inherently against morality and therefore strongly resisted. This includes both right-wing attempts to introduce race-based nationalism and left-wing attempts to introduce safe speech and progressive stacks as commonly accepted conventions.

The Moral Libertarian Argument Against Early-21st Century 'Far-Left'

On why Moral Libertarianism is incompatible with contemporary identity politics

In recent years, much has been said about the divisive radical identity politics that is tearing our society apart. Left-leaning liberals and progressives, who were once reluctant to criticise these movements out of a misguided concern for 'progressive unity', are becoming increasingly frustrated. But most people still don't seem to get the point of these movements. The words of liberals lamenting how American Left views on issues of identity and equality have strayed far from those of Martin Luther King and Barack Obama in recent years have become a refrain among those who have been more awake to the problem. However, putting it this way frames the problem as a misguided development in a movement still otherwise committed to the values of King and Obama. Rather, to put it bluntly, sections of the Western Left have been hijacked by an alien ideology that shares almost nothing in common with historical liberalism.

The Ideology that is sort of Marxist but not quite like the Marxism we are familiar with

The kind of divisive identity politics we are seeing is based on a political ideology, an ideology that is perhaps not yet well understood by the majority of liberals and progressives. Those behind the divisive drama do not even want the same things as mainstream liberals and progressives. In conventional Western politics, we are conditioned to see politics as a spectrum, from 'extremely liberal' to 'extremely conservative'. However, this spectrum presupposes that there are only two main worldviews, which recent events have thoroughly discredited. To put it simply, the ideology behind the recent divisive identity politics looks like this: it is an ideology that believes the only way to change is to tear apart our existing social fabric, because there cannot be real change in liberal reform, no matter what. It is an ideology that believes there is no point in rational debate and changing people's minds, because the playing field will always favor the privileged, no matter what. It is an ideology that believes it's always going to be an us-vs-them world, at least until some kind of revolution, and the only way to progress is for the oppressed to win and the formerly privileged to lose. In this worldview, to achieve social change, the 'oppressed' would have to develop a consciousness of being oppressed, and fight for victory over their 'oppressors'. Such an ideology would have to constantly create conflict so as to make its case for how useless reformist politics is, and to arouse the fighting spirit of its adherents. Therefore, it needs to make the most of every perceived injustice, no matter how insignificant: the value is in the fight, not the issue itself. Hence the pointless culture wars over inauthentic Asian food, or over Beyonce in an Indian dress. This kind of thinking has probably been lurking in the shadows of the extreme left for at least several decades. With rising frustration in society and the ease of spreading ideas via the internet and social media, it now has a substantial audience and support base.

The idea that it would be better for the oppressed to rise up as a group and fight their 'oppressors' as a group, without consideration for individual guilt or lack thereof, is actually not a new idea. It probably originated in the Marxist idea of class struggle, where the working class would develop class consciousness, and come together to struggle against the propertied class, to bring about a revolution and establish a 'dictatorship of the proletariat'. While Marx only intended for his idea to apply to economic classes, this idea has since taken on a life of its own, as ideas often do. After all, economic classes aren't the only fracture lines in society where this model could be applied. This is why, in late identity politics, it has all been about 'group consciousness' and group claims. The similarity of some of the language used in identity politics movements with traditional Marxist language hints at the historical origin of their model of social change. Of course, this is a very illiberal model of change, in that it violates the equality of every individual and the right of every individual to pursue life, liberty and happiness. But radicals, in the true sense of the word, have never quite agreed with America's founding fathers, anyway. This probably explains why some identity politics movements do not see any irony in asking whites to march at the back, for example.

More on the Methods of Radical Identity Politics

Radical identity politics is essentially a distorted form of class struggle politics, and for practitioners of identity politics, much of the time the value is in the struggle itself. In fact, we need to completely drop the illusion that radical identity politics of any form is somehow about controlling thought and behaviour through specific policies or actions: it's not. History has taught us that the most effective way of gaining support for otherwise unpopular and illiberal ideas is when you have a divisive situation, where people feel oppressed, or are in a struggle state of mind. Therefore, for extremists of all stripes, it's really all about creating the struggle. While the free speech we so value is often the first victim, we must not fall for their invitation for struggle. By deliberately aligning oneself against radical identity politics, one can only give fuel to the struggle, which in turn emboldens the growth of identity politics. Instead of being drawn into the proposed 'struggles', we need to re-assert the importance of free speech, but we also need to bring those on both sides of each argument along, and be able to re-assure them that the liberal democratic process, including free speech and the free market of ideas, is a fair one for all.

For Moral Libertarians, there is simply no Common Ground with Radical Identity Politics. Appeasement is also Not an Option.

In the face of divisive identity politics, true liberals who believe in the way of America's founding fathers, Lincoln, King and Obama alike must take a strong stance against it. This is because, first and foremost, the ideology behind radical identity politics is simply incompatible with the values of liberalism, including the equality and autonomy of individuals, the right of every individual to pursue life and liberty for themselves, and democratic governance via peaceful processes. Every time radical identity politics is practiced, it is effectively spitting into the face of liberal ideals.

For committed moral libertarians, radical identity politics is fundamentally a violation of our most basic principle of morality. As moral libertarians, we believe that situations or movements are only morally sound when all individuals have Equal Moral Agency (EMA). While this is an ideal that can't always be met in real life, any deliberate move away from this ideal is to be considered inherently immoral. In radical identity politics, people are often allocated moral agency (e.g. in having a platform to speak or not) in a deliberately unequal way. Furthermore, individuals in supposedly marginalised groups who do not take up the 'fight against oppression' (as dictated by self-appointed movement leaders) are often treated as 'class traitors', and have their moral agency deliberately taken away as a result. Therefore, there is simply no way a committed moral libertarian can accept working with practitioners of radical identity politics under any circumstances. Instead, we must strongly and clearly oppose radical identity politics at all times, as a matter of moral principle.

Proclaiming the Liberal Alternative

The best alternative to radical identity politics is liberalism, with its message of liberty and equal opportunity for all, and treating each individual as independent and equally important rather than as members of a class or group. In a society where the great ideals of liberalism are commonly accepted, there simply will be no place for group-struggle-based divisive identity politics, and the authoritarian control of thought and speech that inevitably comes with it. However, I must stress again that for liberalism to have widespread support, it must be seen as truly serving everyone, and living up to its promises. It must also be seen as a more moral ideology than its rivals.

Therefore, as liberals, we need to abide by the core principles of liberalism, and apply it equally to all sectors of society, majorities and minorities. I believe what makes liberalism different from (and better than) all other ideologies is its commitment to giving everybody equal moral agency. As reformists (rather than revolutionaries, because revolutionary action is incompatible with moral libertarianism), we understand that we won't get there overnight, but in each era of society we try to make things more liberal, for example by upholding everyone's equal right to free speech, by encouraging rational and objective debate of social issues, and just as importantly, by trying to remove discrimination and prejudice using liberal means. As liberals, our historical achievements in social reform include the equality of political rights regardless or race or gender, the end of slavery and segregation, the end of colonialism and the establishment of a system of international diplomacy, and yes, marriage equality. We must not downplay this legacy just because we are currently engaged in a bitter argument over freedom of speech and conscience with the far-left. Especially when these achievements would have been impossible without free speech and the free market of ideas.

The Moral Libertarian Case Against Safe Speech, Progressive Stack and No-Platforming

Free speech has always been a cornerstone of Western society post-Enlightenment. However, several recent developments are threatening this important tradition: the promotion of safe speech, progressive stack speaking systems, and the increasing acceptance of no-platforming. As we will discuss one by one, all these practices are to be regarded as immoral and unacceptable under the Moral Libertarian worldview, where every individual must be granted Equal Moral Agency (EMA) as much as possible.

Safe Speech

Practicing safe speech, according to its proponents, means making sure that all speech is sensitive to the need to avoid psychologically harming minorities. On the surface, it looks like a noble goal. Surely, whenever I say things, I do try my best not to be hurtful to others. However, the problem is that safe speech is generally not just a matter of personal practice, based on personal conscience. It is policed by both activism and peer pressure. Those who are determined to have breached safe speech codes are punished with a variety of social consequences. Therefore, safe speech is actually a form of censorship against free speech.

Since Moral Libertarians demand that every individual must have Equal Moral Agency (EMA), we cannot accept the practice of censoring free speech, even for theoretically noble reasons. Furthermore, our insistence on this point is based in morality: that no individual is anywhere near moral perfection, and therefore no individual has the moral standing to require another individual to submit to them. It also doesn't matter if those demanding submission are in the majority: since all human beings are flawed and imperfect, even the majority's decisions are not guaranteed to always be more morally correct than the lone individual who disagrees. Therefore, the majority shutting down the speech of that lone individual can still be a potential moral wrong. In other words, the majority, made up of flawed human beings, still do not have the moral standing required to be able to shut up the lone dissenting individual. It doesn't even matter if the majority is 100% certain of their moral righteousness: when you are a flawed human being, your '100% certain' still doesn't equate to the Objective Truth.

Now, theoretical arguments are not persuasive for everyone, so let's look at an actual example. While safe speech has most often been argued in the context of preventing racist and homophobic speech, this is only the thin end of the wedge. Already, there have been attempts to use 'safe speech' to justify disallowing people to say that abortion is immoral, and I actually agree that this is the logical conclusion if you uphold the safe speech principles consistently. Therefore, the application of safe speech can (and actually should) mean that we cannot hold discussions about the morality of abortion at all! My point is that, whether you personally think that abortion is morally acceptable or not, shutting down debate on such a controversial issue would amount to oppressive silence for both sides, and a repudiation of what has always been society's consensus on how to deal with controversial issues. Furthermore, thinking about it, many other morality debates can be shut down using similar justifications, leading to society simply putting a lid on every controversial issue. Nothing but total, oppressive silence. Therefore, the undesirability of 'safe speech' is far from only theoretical!

Progressive Stack

Progressive stack systems are speaking systems where disprivileged minorities are given first priority to speak. According to its proponents, progressive stack will give minorities more of a voice. Again, even though the intention is noble, moral libertarians simply cannot accept it. Firstly, the fact that some people are assigned a higher speaking priority already makes progressive stack completely incompatible with the notion of Equal Moral Agency. But even more importantly, progressive stack systems require regulation to work, and those 'regulating' the system will have complete moral agency over everyone else, since they control whether other people are even allowed to speak at all! Where people have been given a higher priority to speak, they will have been granted this privilege by the regulators, and will be pressured to not upset the regulators. Thus the regulators inevitably end up with a high degree of influence over many other individuals' speech. This is clearly not acceptable for somebody committed to Equal Moral Agency and a free market of ideas.

No-Platforming

Finally, the most outrageous form of speech censorship on the rise today is no-platforming. No-platforming refers to the deliberate denial of a platform to speak for one's opponents. Practitioners of no-platforming eschew the tried and true way of changing people's minds with polite and rational debate. Instead, they directly prevent their opponents from speaking up in the first place, for example by pressuring university administrations to cancel appearances, or by shouting over people as they speak. This is, without need for explanation, a flagrant violation of Equal Moral Agency. It is also the metaphorical equivalent of shutting down the marketplace (of ideas) by oppressive force, thus preventing people from 'buying' what they want.

Think about this: what gives anyone any right to no-platform another? As a fundamentally flawed human being, you don't have any more (or less) moral standing than any other human being. You simply don't have the moral standing to prevent another human being from speaking. Isn't that clear enough?

Moral Libertarian Perspective: John Rawls and the Veil of Ignorance

Contemporary liberalism is heavily influenced by the ideas of John Rawls. In particular, his veil of ignorance theory has had a very strong impact on liberal thinking. Essentially, Rawls argued that people should make decisions under a 'veil of ignorance' about their own position in society, for such decisions to be truly impartial and hence offer equal opportunity to everyone. Here, I will argue that the Rawlsean veil of ignorance actually complements the moral libertarian principle of Equal Moral Agency (EMA) very well.

Firstly, a recurrent criticism of liberalism is that its individualistic orientation encourages individuals to be selfish. Liberalism has been characterized by some as a system that encourages individuals to focus on pursuing their self interests. However, if individuals are encouraged to act under the Rawlsean veil of ignorance, they will be making decisions removed from their own self interests. This shows that liberalism, especially a liberalism that is guided by strong moral principles, does not have to be inherently selfish.

Secondly, I would argue that making democratic decisions under the veil of ignorance is effectively the same as upholding the principle of Equal Moral Agency. This is because, under the veil of ignorance where one supposedly does not know where they stand, one would generally make decisions that will not disadvantage people in any given position in society. This means that such decisions would have to adhere as closely as possible to distributing moral agency equally among every individual. Therefore, for those unsure of how to uphold Equal Moral Agency in collective decisions, the veil of ignorance is perhaps the best starting point.

Finally, the Rawlsean veil of ignorance effectively prevents all forms of divisive identity politics. When one is not supposed to know one's identity in society in the first place, how can one practice identity politics at all? The disabling of identity politics also disables a variety of illiberal ideologies, including race-based nationalism, the Oppression Olympics, trans-exclusionary radical feminism (TERF), and neo-Marxist class struggle revolutionary politics (where identity groups replace the economic classes in orthordox Marxism) alike. Hence practising thinking from a veil of ignorance point of view is a good way to ensure we stay true to liberal values and practices.

In conclusion, while the Rawlsean veil of ignorance concept is not the same as the moral libertarian Equal Moral Agency principle, the two are sort of similar, and complement each other very well.

Moral Libertarian Perspective: False Political Maps give us False Promises of Collectivist 'Liberty'

Ever since the classical left-right political axis of the French Revolution became woefully inadequate to describe the variety of existing political platforms, there have been various proposals of two-dimensional models. The most common version, the one that appears to have become the new de-facto standard, involves adding a socially libertarian vs authoritarian scale in the vertical axis, leaving the horizontal left-right axis to economic matters. This is the kind of map that online tests like Political Compass use. The fact that Political Compass has inspired a countless amount of memes from all sides of the political landscape shows the level of common acceptance of this model.

However, what is commonly accepted is not necessarily what is correct. After all, it was commonly accepted that the Earth was flat in the middle ages too! In fact, I have identified one important flaw in map: part of the map cannot practically exist. Which part of the map am I taking about? The part where you can have next to no economic freedom but lots of social freedom, i.e. the bottom left corner in Political Compass. Of course I understand that economic freedom is not perfectly correlated with social freedom. There have been societies which were dictatorships but had lots of economic freedom (e.g. Pinochet's Chile), and there are societies where economic freedom is limited but there is still considerable social freedom (e.g. Western and Northern Europe). But I would argue that, where economic freedom drops to nearly zero, social freedom would also have to drop to nearly zero, as a rule.

Why would that be the case? Because where there is no economic freedom at all, there is simply no individual agency to do anything meaningful at all. When all the property is collectively owned, everyone would need collective permission to be able to do anything with any piece of property. When all the means of production are in government hands, the only people who get to decide what is produced are the rulers. At this point, you need to remember that access to property and means of production are required for almost any meaningful activity. Without my computer I can't be typing this. Without your computer you wouldn't be able to read this. Therefore, in societies where there is no economic freedom, governments end up controlling all social activity by default. They also get to control the pool of ideas, and therefore what people can and cannot think, by default.

As you can see, there really can be no 'bottom left corner' of the political compass. The extreme bottom-left corner, i.e. a 'libertarian socialism' which collectivizes all private property but just doesn't have a 'government' as we know it, does not offer social liberty. In fact, when you think about it, the collectivization of property would practically require some sort of governance. Even if it doesn't look like the kind of government we are used to, it would still fulfil a similar role. And since there will always be people who do not want to be part of that collectivization, the system would need a way to enforce that collectivization too. Therefore, 'libertarian socialism' is, in my opinion, not too different from Stalinist 'authoritarian socialism' in practice. The two-dimensional political maps just give them an opportunity to brand themselves as very different, when in fact they are not so different.

All this reminds us that, as liberals, we need to care about practical outcomes of liberty or lack thereof, rather than just accepting situations that are 'theoretically pro-liberty'.

The Moral Libertarian Case Against Promoting Myths

Moral libertarianism calls for a vision of a genuinely free market of ideas, where individuals with Equal Moral Agency (EMA) can participate in the debate, criticism and improvement of every idea. Of course, such a system would only be functional if there is no deceit. That is, everyone is required to participate in the free market of ideas in good faith, with every individual aiming to contribute to their best ability towards moving things closer and closer to the truth. To achieve this, we need to promote the importance of being sincerely truthful at all times when it comes to discussing big ideas with moral implications.

The Promotion of Myths is Dangerous

People don't always act in good faith, unfortunately. It is not uncommon for people to put ideas forward, not because they believe it will get us closer to the truth, but because they want to provoke certain reactions, to get certain results. The most common form of this would be the person who would say anything to gain attention or to further their career. Even more dangerous would be to promote myths to inspire political action. The first person who explicitly argued for the promotion of myths to generate political action was probably 19th century French thinker Georges Sorel, who believed in using the myth of the General Strike to further class struggle. Mussolini, the father of fascism, was strongly inspired by Sorel. In fascism, it was instead myths of nationalism and race that were used to generate political action, action that would lead to previously unimaginable horrors. The experience of 20th century fascism stands as the strongest reminder of how dangerous it is to promote myths in order to advance political ideology.

However, the promotion of myths do not have to be deliberate. While most people are not as immoral as to promote political myths deliberately, the unconscious promotion of political myths can be just as dangerous. For example, promoting the idea that immigrants are destroying the traditional culture of the country can easily fan racist and ultra-nationalist sentiment, that will be translated into illiberal political action. Another example is the promotion of the false idea that the political centre is continually moving to the right, which is quite common in leftist circles. This idea leads people to falsely believe that they should embrace far-left politics to counter a trend that does not really exist. (I mean, how is our current political centre to the right of the 1950s centre? How is this belief even logical?) The unconscious promotion and propagation of myths most commonly occur in echo chambers, something which we must avoid at all costs.

Nobody is Entitled to Their Own Truth

Another way the promotion of myths can be justified, either consciously or subconsciously, would be through moral relativism. Moral relativism is the belief that each cultural group can have their own version of the truth, and the differing versions of 'truth' are not objectively better or worse than each other. It would follow that whatever a group believed sincerely could be counted as truth by definition, at least for that group. It would then follow that, for example, if a group believes that it is oppressed, it is their truth, and they should have the right to promote and propagate this view with impunity. This actually leads directly to the justification of promoting political myths! After all, many Germans in the 1930s did feel that their race was being oppressed, especially after being fed Nazi propaganda. Failing to critically examine this belief led to the biggest horror of all time. While moral relativism actually arose later, its attitude of allowing subjective feelings to be equated to truths would be in line with what happened in 1930s Germany.

Of course, there is an objective truth, and there is an objective morality, that is not the result of cultural or social construction, and that cannot be altered by social engineering. The fact that people may differ in their interpretation of truth is a function of the limitations of human ability and the flawedness of human existence. Thus, while moral libertarians should uphold the right of individuals to speak out about their sincerely held beliefs without penalty from others, this should stem from recognising that no human being is always right, and that no human being has the adequate moral standing to prevent another from speaking, rather than any kind of moral relativism. Moral libertarianism insists that individuals are entitled to speak up about their most sincerely held beliefs about what the objective truth is. This is, however, very different from the idea that individuals should be entitled to their own truths, regardless of the objective truth.

Moral Libertarian Principles can Resolve Issues Beyond the Limits of Classical Libertarianism

Libertarianism has traditionally relied on the Non-Aggression Principle (NAP) to resolve all issues. The NAP states that nobody can initiate violence against another. In practice, it also means that government authority (and therefore potential violence) in all issues is to be disallowed, except for protection against violent crime and violent destruction of private property. Good as the NAP sounds, more and more people are finding it very inadequate for solving a variety of issues in the modern world.

People have been turning to libertarianism for its apparent fairness, because it is an ideology that treats individuals as individuals with equal standing. In libertarianism, there is no governmental exceptionalism (i.e. the government does not have a right to act beyond the NAP), no structural unfairness or reverse discrimination allowed (e.g. the so-called 'progressive stack'), and no ability to justify such structural unfairness on Orwellian Newspeak. It is therefore refreshing for many. However, the lack of practicality in the application of the NAP ultimately leads many to abandon libertarian ideals.

Ultimately, disallowing violence except for self-defence is an expression of the equal standing of human beings, and it is this equal standing of human beings as individuals that leads to the disallowance of centrally planned economies, reverse discrimination dressed up as social justice, and the like. Therefore, I believe that the principle of Equal Moral Agency (EMA) that moral libertarianism is based on is actually similar to the NAP in spirit, but allows more practical application in a wide variety of areas.

Here are a few examples of what I mean:

Drug Policy

In classical libertarianism, there is simply no scope to have a debate on drug policy at all. The NAP requires that there can be no prohibition against any drug being legally available on a commercial basis. Since the provision of such 'goods' do not involve violence, there can be no government authority (and therefore potential violence) to stop it. However, for most people, this is a woefully inadequate approach to such a controversial and sensitive problem.

On the other hand, the Equal Moral Agency (EMA) approach allows a healthy debate. Does allowing a commercial market for 'recreational' drugs increase or decrease the equality of moral agency? On one hand, it increases the freedom of the individual against government regulation, therefore increasing the equality of moral agency. On the other hand, it allows companies to market addictive and potentially harmful substances for the purpose of making an ongoing profit. You could legitimately argue that, once people are addicted to the product, they certainly don't have Equal Moral Agency to the company selling it.

Animal Rights

Animal rights are another area where libertarianism is often thought to be lacking. Put it simply, classical libertarianism does not allow any animal rights at all, because ill-treatment of animals is not associated with violence between citizens in any way. However, this attitude is seen as repulsive by the vast majority of the general population.

On the other hand, moral libertarianism and the EMA principle is grounded in the need to allow each individual full and equal moral agency, to act out their sincerely held moral vision as much as possible without interference from collective pressure. Since there can be no argument that ill-treatment of animals advance any morally useful purpose, laws banning such actions are not against the EMA principle. Conversely, one can argue that the government, which has the right of rule over the land, has therefore a responsibility to protect the 'natural environmental elements' in the land, and the decision as to how to achieve this goal should be one based on democratic mandate, like all other 'unavoidably collective' issues.

Financial Sector Fraud and Regulation

In classical libertarianism, there isn't much scope for government regulation of the financial sector, because financial transactions are non-violent. However, in recent years, bad practices in the financial sector has led to the ruin of many lives across the world. Just sitting there and saying you can't do anything about it will clearly not be acceptable to many people. On the other hand, the Equal Moral Agency (EMA) approach allows government regulation to clamp down on financial sector fraud and malpractice, to restore customers' equal share of moral agency.

In Conclusion

The principle of Equality of Moral Agency (EMA) is indeed different from the Non-Aggression Principle (NAP), and therefore they don't always produce the same policy conclusions. However, EMA is actually based on the same individualistic and 'morally egalitarian' spirit as the NAP. Using the EMA principle to think about issues fosters the same individualistic, non-biased and non-affirmative attitude as using the NAP, but the EMA allows much more ground to consider issues and points of view that are generally considered important in broader society.

Of course, strict thin libertarians and especially thin libertarian immediatists would strongly disagree with using the EMA in place of the NAP. However, we are not all strict thin libertarians, and when given the choice between NAP-based libertarianism and other conventional ideologies, over 95% of the population would rather choose other conventional ideologies and forego the individualism, objectivity, and anti-tribalism found in libertarianism. The EMA approach of Moral Libertarianism provides an alternative that allows people to embrace these values even if they cannot embrace NAP-based libertarianism.

Printed in Great Britain
by Amazon

26387380R00081